Our Births, Our Stories
Volume 3

Inspirational Birthing
from Communities Around the World

By Heather Baker, Traditional Midwife

To have your birth story or photos added, please email heatherbakermw@gmail.com

Dedication

To the countless moms who were told they were not allowed to do this...
They were insane for risking their lives and their baby's...
For the parents who had no support
For the fathers who knew no different
For those breaking old conditioning
For those wanting to make a change for the better
This book and all my books,

are for you.

CONTENTS

Introduction

The Author, Heather Baker, is a Traditional Midwife who has been attending births since 1996. She currently consults for those who have no access to midwives, travels the world to attend births for those who desire it and she supports mothers and birth workers, for women's birth rights. Heather is also a mother to five children all born at home, four being unassisted. Her support towards unassisted birthing is an endless journey.

Heather Baker has published many books to date including: Home Birth on Your Terms, the Spanish version ~ Parto En Casa, the French version ~ Accouchement à domicile selon vos termes, and Our Births, Our Stories Volume 1 and 2. These were all written after several years of compiling information and a deep desire to educate about unassisted and freebirth options.

Her books quickly sold all over the world. Home Birth on Your Own Terms is the first manual of its kind, teaching how to manage yourself in pregnancy, birth and postpartum, solely on your own.

The Stories series was created to support families wanting to birth naturally. These stories are first hand accounts, from mothers and parents, willing to share their intimate memories with you. These compilations share their voices and experiences, so that you can feel elation in your own future birthing options. What you do in preparation for your mind and body, will greatly affect your life in more ways than you can imagine. Choose for you, not what others think is right for you.

I wish you the most beautiful journey to motherhood, whether it is your first time or your eighth.

Autumn

I am a plus size mom of 4 beautiful babies. 2 girls. 2 boys. During my last pregnancy with my daughter, I was told my weight made me high risk at 27 weeks. I had the same weight in all of my previous pregnancies. I actually haven't gained much of anything.

This statement was coming from a midwife at the place I've been going to for the past 4 years. My 3rd baby with them. It didn't sit right with me, to be told my weight risked me out of the birth I wanted with them. Because of my weight I was not fit to birth with them but I can do so in a hospital setting with them. A hospital setting where I would have to labor on one of the tiny hospital beds and not the big white queen bed I was looking forward to. I wouldn't be able to labor in the pool. I would only be allowed to use the shower in the hallway, not even in the hospital room I would be birthing in. I would have to wear a sheet and walk to the shower in the eyes of everyone there. The humiliation I know I would feel doing so because it would be the 2nd time having to do that.

I left my 27 week appointment to meet my husband in the car, after being checked by the midwife and told everything

1

was great. We had talked about my birth plan and I shared how excited I was to labor in the birthing suite and to labor in the pool... how I was looking forward to it all.

We grabbed lunch and headed back to work. A few hours later I got a call from the midwife. She tells me due to my weight, I cannot birth with them and I have to go to the hospital side and give birth there. They will still support me in the hospital, it just won't be in the midwifery suite like I wanted. She says she is sorry and that I should have been informed sooner but my bmi is just to large for them to have in there. I hung up. Tears in my eyes. Trying to hold them in.

I go to the bathroom and put myself together. Im at work. They can't see me escalated. I try to breathe and calm down. I text my husband real fast that the midwife said I can't birth with them anymore and that I have to birth in the hospital and I don't want to go to them anymore. I walk out of the bathroom and face the rest of my shift. Only a few hours left. I get home and break down, I'm so upset. The birth I wanted feels like it's lost to me. My last baby and what I wanted is gone. My husband suggests we contact all the other local midwives and see if I'm okay to go to them. After all, it's just my weight that makes me high risk. We contact them all. They all say the same thing, my weight is fine and Ican birth with them. Then they get to the pricing. 5 thousand. 6 thousand. 7 thousand. All that would have to be paid in full by 32 weeks. I'm 28 weeks pregnant by this point. That's thousands of dollars we don't have, especially by 32 weeks. We talk about taking out a loan. We were suggested care credit. It just doesn't seem feasible to go into that much debt. I mourn my birth plans. Distraught.

At 30 weeks pregnant I get this idea in my head. Free birth. Homebirth. Have the baby on my terms. I talk to my husband. He's not keen on the idea. I start watching birth videos and sending him all the statistics and reading everything and anything I can. He starts doing research on his own.

He finally starts to agree but with conditions. I have to learn anything and everything, I have to be prepared for anything to happen and have a to go bag for just incase. I agree. Research and preparing became my new hyperfocus. I got everything needed. Tinctures for hemorrhaging, backup clamp for the baby umbilical cord, a tincture of anxiety and stress, magnesium oil for cramps, arnica gel for pain relief, arnica tablets for pain relief as well, Tucks for after birth, medical shears to cut the cord, a bowl for my placenta. I sewed a baby hammock to weigh the baby once she was born, with a hanging scale. Tape measure. I crochet a sunflower tie for her belly. I ordered a kids pool for birthing in. A little fishing net for any clots or anything floating in the water. An adapter for my shower to connect the Rv hose to fill the tub, twinkle lights, washcloths galore. Most importantly, I got the most recommended book, Homebirth On Your Own Terms, A How To Guide on Birthing Unassisted. I read it backwards and forwards and so did my husband. He poured over that thing like it was air. He consulted and tested me on what I read and we talked and discussed everything we could think of for what Ifs.

3

We could do this. We were going to. We've got this. We shared with our families what we were doing. Some of the reactions we got, you would think we had 3 heads each. We reassured them we had this. It's fine. Thank you for your concerns. We moved on. I didn't want it in my headspace. It was a no fear zone. Matthew asked that I just attend the midwife visits up until the birth so that way he can make sure me and baby were fine and he would be fine birthing at home. It was our compromise and I agreed.

Fast forward to September 13th.
I awake for the day with tightening cramps low in my uterus. I am 41 weeks and 2 days pregnant with our daughter.

It's 6:30 am and I am getting my oldest daughter up for school and the rest of my children up for the ride and breakfast. I get that all taken care of and still have tightening pains. They aren't to painful but they are noticeable. I take note of the time between them, about 45 minutes or so between them. I think maybe today is the day she joins us.

Time passes us and it's 8 am. I go lay down with the boys still occasionally have the tightening. Matthew arrives home around 9 am and I have a midwife appointment to hear baby's heartbeat and confirm she's still heads down as well as a chiropractor appointment. By the time we reach the midwife, the tightening has turned into some pretty good contractions and are about 25 minutes apart. The midwife asked if I wanted to be checked and I was curious so I went ahead and had her check my cervix. I was dilated at a 4 and 70% effaced and she said my waters were bulging. I think to myself that must be why I'm feeling so much extra pressure down there. I head out and go to the store with Matthew and the boys to grab some stuff for our oldest daughter's birthday and some herbal books I had seen online and wanted to pick up.

I have to stop every little bit around the store to breathe through the contractions. They are starting to get more consistent about 15 minutes now apart. We finish up at the store and head to my chiropractor appointment. It's 12 pm now. By the time we get there, the contractions are about 10 minutes apart. I tease with my Chiropractor that I'm tempting fate getting adjusted in labor like this. I get adjusted and have a contraction in the office. They sent me on my way. No heat and stem since I'm in labor and have an hour drive home.

I check out and have another contraction on my way out the door. Matthew laughs when I make it to the car and teases me because I didn't take long at all… I must really be in labor. We grab lunch quick and I devoured it. It was so good. Then we make our way towards home, an hour away.

I call my mom and tell her I'm in labor and she says she will prepare to leave work. She texts us and says the baby won't be here for hours, probably midnight. I laugh. I know it won't be long at all. I call my mom back and tell her we will get Arya from school.

When we are about 20 minutes from home I call the school and ask for our daughter to be prepared to leave early. We make it to the school and my contractions are about 5-8 minutes apart. She complains in the car she missed recess. We laugh and say she's about to get her sister. She cheers up. I text my friend, who's going to act as my Doula, that I'm in labor and she asks are you sure this is it? I confirm. I know within a bit she will be here. She says it will be a playdate with the kids and will be here in an hour and brings her 2 daughters.

Matthew starts airing up the birthing pool and getting water boiled on the stove to sterilize everything. I start cleaning. I sweep and mop our bedroom in between contractions. Clean up the living up, the bathrooms. My mom hangs back and chills out with the kids watching movies in the bedroom with them trying to keep them from diving into the birthing pool. My friend arrives and we introduce our kids. It's the first time we have actually met in person. It was a great way to have a playdate. A Birth and kids playing. Quite memorable that's for sure.

It gets to be around 3 something. I don't really know the time. I start feeling the surges more and tell Matthew I'm ready to get into the birthing pool and start laboring in there. He checks the temp and starts cycling out the water so it's still nice and hot for me. I relax in the pool. I love the heat. The pain is less in there. My body tells me to go to my hands and knees. Matthew reminds me to breathe and I ask him to put a hot rag on my lower back. I breathe and my mom says moan into it. It helps.

When the contractions stop I sit back down and rest and relax. With every contraction Matthew put pressure on my lower back. I put on a homesteading video on the TV in the background, to distract me earlier, my friend teases me. It doesn't last long until I change it to some laboring music. I start feeling panicky and ask Matthew for some rescue remedy. He gets it for me. My nerves calm down. A few more times it happens. I know I'm in transition. My mom says she's going to run home real quick. I panic and start to get tears in my eyes and beg her to stay and Matthew gets me more rescue remedy. She stays. More contractions happen.

I feel the urge that I have to poop. I know my body and it's telling me she will be here soon. She's almost here. It's 430ish. My older children are on my bed watching me labor. I ask my friend to film. She mishears me... I try to correct her and say film but my brain is distracted with a contraction and she finally gets what I'm trying to say just as I say she's coming. And out she came out in 2 pushes. I grab her out of the water and pull her to my chest. Its 4:39 pm.

I panic a little because she's en caul, with the sac around her. I break it open. Her face squished at me and she opens her eyes and looks at me and her mouth gapes at me. I panic thinking she's inhaled water and start asking for the aspirator. Matthew puts a towel on her to keep her warm. I realize she's fine. She was just breathing and adjusting. She was fine. Didn't need the aspirator.

I clean off the sac from her head and just stare in awe. That I did it. I birthed my baby. I'm in shock honestly. It feels unreal. I'm so happy. I keep her warm and we change the towels on her. My placenta starts to come and

7

Matthew thinks I'm hemorrhaging a bit so he gives me some tincture to help.

My placenta takes what seems like forever to come. My energy gets a little low. I'm in the birthing pool still. Just holding her up above the water. We keep changing her towel to keep her warm as she nurses. About an hour passes and my uterus contracts. It's still not enough to get my placenta to dislodge. It's still half inside of me, half out. The cord is short so I can't move her without pulling the cord, so we just stay for a bit longer. Matthew keeps giving me raw honey to boost my energy. It helps alot.

I suggest we get us to the bed. Matthew and my friend help me up. He holds and supports my placenta for the transfer. The transfer was enough for my uterus to contract and release the last bit of the placenta and into the bowl it goes! They help wrap her into a nice warm towel from the dryer. Matthew grabs a hot wash rag and cleans me up from the blood. Telling me good job that I did it.

More time passes and the cord is no longer pulsing. It's limp and white. Matthew grabs the sunflower tie and ties it around her cord. My mom film's as he cuts the cord. He did a great job. We bundle her back up for a bit. She wants to nurse more. Carissa suggests we weigh her since she pooped. Don't want her losing anymore birth weight before we weigh her. I clean up her poop then we all work to weigh her in the scale I made. 8 lbs 3 oz.

I put on her first cloth diaper on. Snapping down the umbilical cord snap and put it on around her. Man she's so tiny and thin around her hips. It looks huge on her but with a few snap adjustments it's on.

I'm so greatful. I held her while Matthew and Carrisa work to get the birth pool all cleaned up and put away so the kids don't play in the birth pool. Matthew puts the placenta into the fridge and my mom gives me more blankets to put her in so she's warm. We celebrate as a family and relish in the beauty of her.

Astrid Oliva Marie Borders
8 lbs 3 oz 20 inches long
September 13th 2022
4:39 pm.
Our beautiful freebirthed little mermaid born en caul.

Jorian Shepherd Phelps

3-16-15

For this birth, my fifth birth, all I wanted was something different. I wanted a completely different birth experience; I wanted to know what it was like to labor slowly throughout the daytime hours. I wanted my kids awake and part of the experience. I also wanted a boy after four girls. I prayed earnestly for these things through the entire pregnancy.

My "due date," March 6th, came and went. On the morning of March 16, 2015, I began light contractions around 6 am. I was able to sleep through them until about 7:30 am. I called Drew to tell him I didn't want to get my hopes up but I was thinking today was the day. They were about twenty minutes apart when I sent him to run some errands with the kids. When I was up and moving, they picked up to every 7-10 minutes. I cleaned my house trying to keep busy and keep things moving along. When Drew got home I decided I needed to rest, believing it was going to be a longer labor. We all went and got into bed and watched a movie; I slept in between contractions that slowed to every twenty minutes.

I got up around noon and decided to get things moving along so I got in the tub in hopes to relax and speed things back up. Nadia (7) sat by my side and wrote down my contractions and kept adjusting my water temperature. After about thirty minutes with some very close, intense contractions I decided to get out and sit on the toilet. While sitting there, contractions picked up more. I had Drew there to support me.

Contractions never really got consistent, Drew was trying to encourage me to move to the bedroom to get more comfortable. I was trying to make progress to move but wasn't able to stand up in between contractions so I kept holding off. Alida (2) kept running in and out, not sure what was going on. The big girls (5 and 7) were playing on Drew's computer in the next room.

I did not realize how close we were to the end. I began feeling incapable and overwhelmed so I began crying out to Jesus to help me through; once I started doing this, I really felt a release of anything holding me back and a sense of relaxation take over my placenta area. Nine minutes passed from when I had my last contraction and in that instant my water broke, I started pushing and he was coming out! It was all fetal ejection reflex taking over. He came gushing out instantly and Drew had to throw me over his shoulder to catch the baby from going into the toilet, he was so big that he wouldn't have fit anyway!

Alida ran in just in time to see it all take place, then ran back out again. He was born at 1:28pm. While Drew was holding the brand new wet baby, I was over his shoulder and I said, "I need to stay here for a minute, I can't move yet," and he said it was fine, he could stay like that for as long as I needed.

Finally, I was able to sit back down and he called the girls in so Ivy (5) could tell us the gender, it was her appointed job. She got to say, "it's a BOY!!" and she and Nadia (7) threw their arms around each other and started jumping up and down. I moved into the bedroom where Nadia cut the cord and we waited and waited and waited for the placenta.

Contractions finally picked back up and I pushed it out two hours after his birth. Jorian Shepherd Phelps was a very content baby right from the start; he wasn't phased by the chaos around him. He weighed just over 10 pounds and was 21.5 inches long.

We were so very blessed and happy. It took a while to replace "she" and "her" with "he" and "his," since we had four girls prior to this little guy.

Alida told everyone who came to visit that "mommy poop baby boy" … with grunting and pushing motions.

Alastor's birth story

I want to share my son's birth story to empower and inspire all women. I hope that this helps show that we can do anything from growing babies to birthing them, because we are warriors.

12/30 around 1 PM: I had a little bloody show while I was peeing. I noticed some blood and tinged mucus on the toilet paper. This is when I started to kinda let people know it could be soon, but that it also could be a false alarm because I had been having prodromal labor for 2 weeks prior. I continued to have some blood on my toilet paper throughout the rest of the day and kept an eye on it.

12/30 4 PM: I went to take a nap on my heating pad with some mild cramping because I figured I should get some rest now in case I couldn't later.

12/30 5 PM: I woke up with strong "cramps"/ contractions and decided to try to walk them off. They were about 2 minutes long, then I would have a 10 minute break in between. I would walk one off then bounce on my ball in between for a few hours until my ball started to become unbearable.

12/30 8:30 PM: That was when I decided it was time to take a bath to relax, while my partner set the kids up to leave the house and organized/prepared everything for the birth. The bath helped relieve the pain of my contractions a bit but once I got back out, it was back to the same old routine.

12/30 9 PM: I knew I couldn't keep walking much longer after I got out of the tub. I needed a new way to work through everything. My contractions were 5 minutes long and 3 minutes apart at this point. I started to vomit and leaning over the trash can felt like a good position. So, I went on hands and knees and bent my upper body over my yoga ball. I rocked my hips back and forth for about 5 hours while my partner brought me fluids and rubbed my back. I puked a few times. I put pillows under my knees because they hurt worse than my contractions. I just got in the zone and rode every wave. The TV was on playing a few movies and I didn't even pay any attention.

12/31 2 AM: I decided to take another bath. It helped relax my muscles but the contractions were hard to deal with because I wasn't able to move around. So, it was very short lived.

12/31 3 AM-ish: After I got out of my second bath, I could feel my contractions getting stronger and they were waxing and waning. They were never fully gone but there were periods when they were more dull. Then they would be sharp for a good amount of time. I wasn't able to track anything at this point and I was just breathing and moving side to side bent over my ball like before. I told my partner to make sure the pool was completely filled and ready because things were picking up/becoming less and less comfortable. While he was getting that done, my water broke on top of my pillows. I worked through a few very strong contractions, trying to make sure I didn't give birth right there as the ejection reflex was starting.

Soon we were up and moving to the pool, slowly. I could feel a lot of pressure while I was trying to walk with my partner's guidance. I knew he was close. I got into the pool on my hands and knees and my partner got in behind me to support me and catch the baby. I remember telling him how I had to keep my legs positioned in KICO (knees in, calves out) as much as possible to help keep my pelvis open. I had a few contractions that naturally moved the baby and in between them I was visualizing my baby down the canal, while also using breathing techniques. I had maybe 3 more contractions with the natural reflex to push and his head was out. I wanted to wait a second before I pushed out the rest of his body. After a few seconds, I pushed his body out into my partner's hands. Baby then proceeded to cry and pee into the birth pool.

Alastor Alderon Ash was born at 3:40 AM on 12/31/21 weighing 6 pounds 9 ounces and 17.7 inches long

Elizabeth

Jonathan Alan Yair

Before getting pregnant I decided that I wanted an unassisted pregnancy. It just felt like what I was supposed to do. I found out I was pregnant very early in the pregnancy, like I always do. The only monitoring I did was check my weight a few times throughout pregnancy.

I was due 4/2 but in the days leading up to labor I let the baby know I was ready, whenever he was ready to come. I would tell baby how I couldn't wait to hold and cuddle him. I couldn't wait to smell his hair.

We usually go to the park every weekday for most of the day but on 3/22 I decided I wanted to rest instead. I spent the day laying on the couch and we binge watched netflix. Around 6pm I got the urge to clean so I got the kitchen, front room, and bathroom clean before putting our kids to bed. We got them to sleep and I fell asleep.

I woke up at 1:30AM wet, so I went to the bathroom and realized it was my water. I sat in the kitchen watching netflix, snacking on carrots and ranch, and waiting for my contractions to start. At 2:11AM I had my first contraction. I then had 5 more contractions 4-5 minutes apart each.

Then they stopped.

At 2:40AM I decided to lay down and get some rest while I could because I would have a busy day ahead of me. I laid down but we cosleep with our 2 and 4 year olds and they were so close I was worried I was going to leak fluid on one of them so I got back up. I watched some more netflix while snacking until 4AM but decided to double up the towels because I really needed some rest. I slept until 5 when I needed to pee and change towels because the ones I had were soaked.

I was able to sleep again from 5:30-6:50AM when thunder outside woke me up. I went to the bathroom and then to the kitchen to brush my teeth. At 6:54AM I had my first real contraction. After that contraction, they started coming every 2 minutes. My 10 year old was rubbing my back and telling me it would be okay through my contractions. My 14, 9, and 7 year old were also awake. At 7:11AM I sent my 14 year old to wake my husband up so he didn't miss the birth because I could tell it was very close.

At 7:19AM our team green baby was born into mine and hubby's arms while I was standing in our kitchen. Our 10 year old was in the kitchen and our 14, 9, and 7 year old came in right after when they heard a bunch of fluid hit the floor. Baby cried and our 6, 4, and 2 year old woke up and came out to see. I checked the gender and announced to everyone that we had another boy.

30 minutes later I delivered the placenta in the bathroom by doing gentle pushes. Me and the baby then made our

way to the couch and laid down and cuddled for hours. At 1:20pm we decided it was time to go ahead and cut his umbilical cord. We then weighed our baby. He was 7lbs 5oz. We've been enjoying the last few weeks with this sweet boy. We finally decided on a name 2 weeks later..

He was born on Francisco's (our first freebirth baby) 2nd birthday.
Jonathan Alan Yair
March 23, 2022 @ 7:19AM
7lbs 5oz. 20 1/4in

Jennifer

Homebirth story of Jace

So before I tell my homebirth story I wanted to give a little background on my older children's births. I wouldn't be where I am today without those experiences. My first son was born in 2016. I was young and trusted doctors. I didn't educate myself at all. Had a totally normal and healthy pregnancy but I was induced with cervadil and pitocin at 40+6 because the doctor didn't want to let me go over 41 weeks. I got an epidural, then stalled at 7cm. It ended in an emergency c section because baby's heart rate went down three times. At the time I didn't realize if I hadn't been unnecessarily induced, I probably would've had a normal vaginal birth.

I find out I was pregnant with my second in November 2019. I was interested in homebirth but nervous because it would be my first vaginal birth. Halfway through my pregnancy I started seeing an OB. He was "supportive" of a vbac but still talking about the possibility of induction if I went over 40 weeks. That didn't sit well with me so I quit going to that OB and decided I was going to have a homebirth but it would have to be unassisted.

I ended up going past my due date. I was having

contractions for a couple days before I was in active labor. I labored at home until I was in transition. The pain was unbearable and I decided to go to the hospital in hopes of getting some sort of pain relief. When I arrived at the hospital, the nurse and doctor on call said that they don't do vbacs there. My husband knew that I absolutely didn't want another c section so he then said "we'll leave and drive an hour to a hospital that does." The nurse then says "Well at least let me check you before you go." We agree and find out I'm 8, almost 9. She's reaching super high up there and I thought it was strange. Then when she was done, I go to move and my water breaks. I'm pretty sure she did it purposely so we couldn't leave.

We were taken to a room and the doctor tells me multiple times that I needed to have a c section. His reasoning was they couldn't call in an anesthesiologist in the case of an emergency c section. If we agreed to a c section, then the anesthesiologist could come. This made no sense to me. I knew that my dreams of having a vaginal birth would most likely be over if I agreed to that so I just firmly told him no every time they asked. The doctor asks to check me again and tells me it's time to push. He kept telling me to push with all that I had because they couldn't find the baby's heart beat. I believe he had just gone below the monitor and it was nothing to be afraid of, but they still used it as a scare tactic.

The doctor then forcefully ripped me open as I was pushing, causing me to have a second degree tear. I busted all the blood vessels in my face and eyes from pushing so hard. I knew then, if I had another child, I would never step foot in a hospital again. That experience also opened my husband's eyes to the horrors of hospitals.

So now onto my redeeming amazing home birth story…

I had been having irregular contractions since the night of 12/7. Around 1:45am on 12/9 the contractions were hurting bad enough that I couldn't sleep through them. I labored in my room, changed positions on my bed, moving and bouncing on my yoga ball. Once that stopped providing some relief I decided to take a warm bath. I didn't stay in the bath long so I went back to my room. With each contraction I kept telling myself I'm closer to meeting my baby. I also prayed. I was surrendering, knowing that god gave my body the amazing ability to be able to do this. Putting my full trust in him that myself and baby would work together just as we were meant to.

I kept reminding myself to "not tense up, breathe, don't tense up, breathe…" after every contraction. Around 6am, I started throwing up in the bathroom from the unbearable pain (I knew I was in transition)

I woke up my husband to start applying counter pressure. He was barely awake and falling asleep in between each contraction but still doing a great job with the counter pressure. I honestly don't know if it helped or not with the pain but it did help me kind of take my mind off the intensity. My contractions at this point were every minute, one right after the other so I was hoping it was almost over. I hadn't lost my mucus plug or had bloody show, so I was a little nervous we might have a while to go.

7:30 I was kneeling on the side of my bed and my husband said that I was bleeding a little. He then takes a picture to show me what's going on. It's almost time I thought, for some the bleeding might've been scary but for me it was reassuring that we were going to be meeting our baby boy soon. I then decided I was going to gently start pushing with each contraction. My water hadn't broken yet but fluid started trickling out with each push. My husband was right behind me and I said, "Babe I'm probably peeing on you, sorry." He said "No, I think that's your water breaking."

All of a sudden I felt the baby's head shoot down into the birth canal. It was crazy. I didn't experience that with my first vbac baby. I tell my husband I can feel the baby's head moving down and he's coming. Next push my mucus plug comes out. Next push, top of baby's head to his eyes were out. My husband says, "Babe, I can see his eyes! You're doing a great job."

I decided when I started pushing that I was going to go slow and steady to try and avoid tearing. I instinctively get into a runner's stance, one more push and his head was out. On the next one, his whole body came out. My husband caught him. It was silent for a second. He's then rubbing the baby's back and trying to suction him. Then the most beautiful sound... baby starts crying. I ask hubby what time it is and he tells me 7:45. We then maneuver the cord and I turn around so I can hold my baby. All I could think was, 'Wow, we did it! We actually did it!' It was such a high, like I've never felt before.

About 30 minutes later, I delivered the placenta and my

husband cut the baby's cord. The overwhelming peace of being in the comfort of our own home and being able to cuddle up in my own bed, take everything in, was so incredible.

I had no tearing this time and when my baby was a week old, I didn't have any pain at all. The recovery has been 100% better than any of my other births.

My son is now 6 months old and I'm honestly still in awe of the experience and that I was able to do this. My husband was an amazing support. I wish I would have chosen this for all of my children's births. Thank you for letting me share my story!! I hope that it can help and inspire other moms.

Paige

Randi Dobrich

A little backstory. 11 years ago we lost our daughter, Sofija, a few hours after birth due to preterm labor at 23 weeks. We then had 4 amazing little boys; Blake, Brice, Baryn and Bhodi. 2 of the boys were also born premature. Each pregnancy I had a goal... my dream birth, in the water. Each time it was taken from me.

This time we did a wild pregnancy with the exemption of going to a boutique sono place. We chose to have a freebirth if I could make it to 37 weeks.

It was an emotional, long pregnancy. We don't find out the gender but I had this pull this time to find out. When we found out it was a girl, I struggled. I truly believe God put that pull on me to find out so I could prepare myself mentally and emotionally to have another girl. Each day that I went over my 'due date' I was shocked. I just wanted to meet my little girl so bad.

At 41.1 weeks, I woke up at 7:30am feeling off. I went to the bathroom and sat there for a bit. Wiped and saw my bloody show. I knew this was finally it. I called my sister to come over.

At 7:45 I had my first contraction and it was powerful! I told my 10 year old to fill the bathtub up. I got in the tub at 7:50 when I had my second contraction, even more powerful than the first. I had two small, back to back contractions at 7:52. At 7:55 I felt pressure, reached down and felt my water break in my hands. That was pretty neat to feel!

My sister pulled in the driveway right then. Talk about perfect timing. 7:58, another contraction where I could feel her head starting to crown, next push her head was out. 1 more push and she was born in the water right into my husband's hands. I pulled her up, unwrapped the cord that was loosely around her neck, rubbed her back and heard that beautiful cry. I instantly started to cry. My baby girl was born safely at home surrounded by her big brothers, dad and aunt. It was beautiful, amazing and powerful.

This pregnancy was a surprise, and I struggled with the gender for a long time. But she is just the perfect addition to our family and completes us. Our first and last being a girl is so special to us.

After my previous births in hospitals and birthing centers, this one was very redeeming for me. I got to make the choices. I got to be in full control of my body. I finally got to have my dream birth! Our bodies are absolutely amazing when we fully surrender and trust ourselves!

7lbs, 20 inches long.
Bayli Grace

She has 4 big brothers to protect her and her sister in heaven, who is watching over us.

Nisha's Birth story

My birth story begins with my first pregnancy. I was on autopilot, like many of us are. I signed up for the regular industrialized care. Waiting 2-3 hours to see an OB-GYN for 5 minutes was definitely off putting. It led me to start researching other options and I found a birth centre in another city. I truly believed that I would have a more natural and collaborative birth experience. In many ways, this was true. In any other hospital, I would have been worse off.

At 36 weeks I moved to Kochi and waited for my baby to come. Around 38 weeks into my pregnancy, my amniotic sac started leaking. At that point I thought, labour was imminent, but my baby and body had other plans. My care provider put me on antibiotics even though I showed no sign of infection. I did an ultrasound which showed that my baby was doing fine, though water levels were a bit low. My water continued to leak for 2 weeks after that and around 40+1 day, the midwives suggested I give castor oil a shot, because my body was "clearly" not going into labour.

The castor oil seemed to work initially. I felt my contractions come and go, I was also inexperienced so I went to the birth centre sooner than I ought to have gone. What followed was chaos. Squats, steps, trying different positions, on the loo, off the loo. Whew! I was also submitted to extremely painful cervical checks to check for dilation. I remember thinking that if I died then, it would be ok, as the pain was so intense. I remember exhausted remarks from my midwife whether I would be there the next day too, which definitely is not something a labouring person needs to hear. In general I could sense the midwives whispering in the background, which was a huge distraction. I was made to walk around the common areas where there were other clients waiting for their appointments.

Finally a lot of "Push Push Push…" during pushing, directions to move to the bed, push some more on my back and then all fours and finally he was born. He was born and placed on the bed.

The following events I don't remember happening but my husband did- Baby was born, eyes open still connected to the placenta but not breathing, the midwife gave him a few puffs mouth to mouth resuscitation and he started breathing.

At this point I was just glad my labour was over and my baby was with me. At one point my mum had come to see us, Omar had stepped out of the room and my midwife in her exact words said, " Nisha, you must not be angry with me, I had to give you a bit of pitocin to speed things up, as the baby was not descending due to the cord pulling against the leg." What she said honestly didn't come as a surprise as I thought I overheard something about them doing this while I was labouring. At that time, shortly after the birth, I thought the interventions that were done were justified and had "saved" me.

The postpartum care after Vedh's birth was really lovely and I have only good things to say about the birth centre staff that came to visit me at home. My mum was with me for a good 3 months after the baby was born so my postpartum period was wonderful and relaxed.

Omar and I knew we wanted Vedh to have a sibling and close together in age. I was quite connected to my cycles and knew when I was fertile so becoming pregnant again happened quickly. This time around there was a birth centre that had opened in Bangalore itself, so I thought I would just stay here. Something never quite felt right and leaving the comfort of my home to head to another city mid pandemic just felt counter intuitive. I started my care with them, which was ok. This time around I was armed with the knowledge of what birth was actually like and knew what I would do differently with my care provider.

One day I get a call from them that the birth centre is not going to be doing any births as they are community midwives and not certified nurses or some such issue. This time around I would make sure I would have more control over my birth. I found myself pulled into the wonderful social media world of the autonomous sovereign free birthers. I listened to more than 200 birth stories and they moved me. I cried, laughed and was inspired by their stories. They opened my eyes to what we as humans are actually capable of and how much we have screwed it up. It blew my mind, how we as women have allowed this total disempowerment to continue for so long.

From around halfway through my pregnancy, I knew it in my bones that I had to birth in power, that I could trust no one if I wanted to birth the way I wanted. So I called up my midwife and told her that I wouldn't be coming. I even jokingly mentioned to her that I might freebirth, to which she said, "I don't know if that's a good idea... what if the baby is born and doesn't breathe?" Though I am sure her intentions were good, she just did not trust the true nature of birth itself.

To birth like the true mammal that we are, stepping out of my home would be the 1st intervention, and I wanted none. I wrote my birth visualization, listing out exactly how I wanted my birth to be. I held that plan close to my heart. I didn't do any more scans, I decided to just care for myself in a way that would make me happy. I did massages, Biodynamic craniosacral therapy and acupressure to just keep my body feeling light and full of energy.

I knew I needed one person with me during the birth, a feminine energy that would hold space and be there for me if required. I knew only one person who I would ask and I knew in my heart she would agree. So I called a my doula friend (R) to be with me and I thanked my stars that she agreed to partner with me on this. That really sealed it. I was so excited to see how things would unfold.

I spent the rest of my pregnancy days, learning about the

essentials of birthing at home. I found a Holistic doula and midwife Tapasya, who shared my excitement for how I was planning my birth. My husband and I enjoyed our calls with her, learning about DIYing the birth, learning about birth emergencies, stocking up on homeopathics, and home birthing equipment. I told no one about my plans, only my husband and mother knew how I intended to give birth and they were very supportive as they trusted me.

I then played the waiting game, I spent time with my son, went for walks, did some stretches whenever I felt like it, bounced on the ball and danced to the music that I had collected to play during labour. My due date came and went. I knew it would definitely go over 40 weeks, so no big deal. I had started feeling prodromal labour on and off for 2 weeks now, so I knew something was happening, I just had to let go and wait.

A day shy of 42 weeks, I saw my mucus plug come out at around 6 am and I was super excited! I told my husband that something might happen that day, but not to get too excited as it could still be days before anything happened. Around 8 am, I could feel surges on and off now, coming in quite regularly. I just stayed in bed, listening to my meditations and mantra music. I walked around, eating biryani for lunch while going through the surges. I called my doula and told her what was happening and asked her to get here only in the evening, past 6 pm, as I didn't see anything happening before that. Everything was going just nice and easy.

As the sun set, I felt things slowly pick up, the intensity slowly building. The whole house is in complete darkness except for one lamp in the corner and 2 candles. At around 8.30-9pm I wanted to get into my room. It was already prepped for birth. I had a mattress on the floor with waterproof sheets and old bedsheets on top. It was just R and I in the room at this point. I wanted no one else. I laboured on the floor, the bed and the bathroom. Lunging on the ball or goddess squatting at the foot of my bed. R's massages during each surge helped with the pain.

My amniotic sac had not broken. I remembered in my Birth Visualization, that I wrote at the very start of my pregnancy… my vision of how I wanted my birth to unfold and very clearly I had written that my water bag would rupture only at the time of birth. Even R remembered and gently asked me to give permission to my bag to give way. I roared my permission, at this point. At each surge, I would hold on to the edge of my bed with both my hands and twerked. (You read that right) I twerked my body rhythmically up and down, which was great pain relief. It was in this moment of true surrender of my body, my cries and tears, that I suddenly stopped and my baby just took over.

I looked R in the eye and told her, "Baby is coming." Suddenly there was no more pain, just the smooth sensation of my girl flowing down. I very calmly got on top of my mattress in a lunge and told R, that the baby is coming and she can help receive and place the baby on the mattress under me. Just as I said this, the head was born and in the next breath she flew out. She had a nuchal arm, so she had

32

her palm on her chin while the cord was tucked under her arm, as if she was thinking some deep thoughts. The cord was around her neck which I unraveled and then saw that she was indeed a girl.

Wow, both R and I were simply ecstatic. I just took a while on the bed to just feast all my senses on my baby after which Omar and my mum came to take a look at her.

Clean up was super quick, old sheets were binned and that was the only clean up necessary. I spent the next hour or so in bed, just marveling at everything. When it was time for the placenta to come out, almost an hour after the birth, I switched lights off again, sat on a bowl in the toilet and whoosh she came out whole and beautiful. R helped clean up and we did some placenta prints while chatting about the birth.

I had some pretty intense afterpains and was starving! Omar got me some warm chicken curry and toasted bread which I devoured, followed by madeleines for dessert. A splendid after birth meal.

My postpartum was so joyous, mostly because of how proud I was of trusting my body and listening to my intuition. What a wonderful way to be born, at home, surrounded by loved ones. My daughter and I will always have this shared experience and hopefully she will also grow to trust her voice and have power over her body. In a country like India where patriarchy still has a very strong hold on the lives of its daughters, we desperately need a rewilding of the feminine, one birth at a time, one mother at a time.

Namiko Sade May

My name is Anna Emlano, I'm 21 years old and from New York. The freebirth facebook group and book, Homebirth On Your Own Terms inspired me to plan my first ever free birth with my second baby. This happened in the early morning of November 2nd, 2020. I wrote my story not even 24hrs after she was born.

I did it!! Everything escalated so fast. Caught her myself. Namiko Sade May born at 12:30 ish. 41 Weeks.

Lost my mucus plug 10/31 and more pink chunks all day 11/1. Contractions were consistent around 7pm. Every 7 minutes they would come and it would feel pretty intense. 8pm I thought I should take a shower, then get my 20 month old to lay down with me and his dad, so we could get some rest. By 10pm, my son was asleep and me and dad were trying to sleep too.

11 pm my son woke up and did not want to go to sleep. Contractions were horrible at this point so I decided to take him in the hallway and sit on my yoga ball. Pressure was so intense. I knew I had to poop so I was trying to get it out. Contractions were coming quick and I just yelled

and moaned through them, but I felt great in between contractions. Dad was sleeping. I go in the bathroom, shut the door to try and poop. (my son stayed in the hall playing with toys and watching his show). I could only poop a little. I felt my vagina to see if I lost any more plug and I felt the bag bulging right at the opening. I was like, there is no way she already descended. I call for dad but he doesn't hear me.

I get in the tub. At this point, I'm so excited, thinking she'll be born en caul. Im think, "ok just wait for the next contraction and she'll be out." I feel again and the bag isn't there. I'm like,. I see big kicks in my stomach. I'm like... HOW? Did I even feel the bag??? Am I tripping??? So I reach up with one finger as far as I can and feel movement. At this point I was so confused and done. I was about to get out and go to sleep.

Contractions come and I was like, I need to poop in this water now. So I got on all fours in the tub and push. A little turd comes out and I feel the bag explode. Vernix chunks fill the tub and I'm just like whatttt is this? what is happening? Then my body just starts violently pushing and I feel her hair crowning. At one point I had to stop and say out loud, "SLOW down and breathe." I couldn't slow down and her head popped out quick. Then her body flew out seconds after. I thought I tore but I guess I didn't! She was covered in vernix!!! I screamed for her dad about 10 times until he came rushing in, half asleep and so confused. This was around 12:50AM 11/2

(trigger warning)

I may have hemorrhaged. I definitely bled much more than I expected. After she came out, the tub was so filled with blood. I didn't panic. We waited about 15-20 mins before taking angelica to help the placenta come out. It came with a few big clots, and a lot of blood. Not gonna lie, I was worried but felt okay. I couldn't call an ambulance for many reasons, so I was determined to get things under control.

I drank orange juice and tons of water with Afterease tincture and tried to compress my uterus down. I moved to the toilet where I felt so dizzy like, oh my god, I am gonna pass out. I just breathed deeply and focused on staying awake and compressing my uterus firmly. I had dad get me the left over wings from the fridge and he fed them to me. I feel like that helped me a lot.

I stayed on the toilet and nursed babe for over an hour. I still felt weak by the time I got up but wasn't bleeding really except for a few drops.
I feel well now. It's 10:30am. I feel like in that moment, I may have needed assistance but I'm really grateful I was able to get bleeding under control.

Nola's FreeBirth Story

This is the story of my daughter Nola's free birth.

After I had my son, I knew I never wanted to birth in a hospital again. I had considered doing a home birth with him, but made the ignorant mistake of trusting a surgeon to support my choice for a natural birth. So once I became pregnant with Nola, I established care with a midwife. She was kind, and natural minded and very respectful, but something in me called me to an unassisted birth. I had toyed with the idea a lot, and even brought it up to Olijawan (my fiancé) and he said he didn't like the idea of it, and it scared him. But I still felt confident. Fast forward, I was 38 weeks pregnant, and I get a call from my midwife, she said she was no longer accepting my insurance and I would have to pay out of pocket for my delivery, and I just knew that was my sign. Why would I pay for someone to sit there and watch me do what I could do myself.

So I was set, I would be birthing unassisted, I called Olijawan, told him the situation and he just said, I trust you. That was all I needed to hear. And now we wait.

April 20th, I had been experiencing contractions on and

off for a few days. I was getting frustrated and tired, and overall just done with being pregnant, aren't we all at 39 weeks 4 days? We had gone for a walk around the park, and easily walked 2 miles. I curb walked for like 30 minutes. I just wanted this damn baby out.

On the way home Omari (my son) fell asleep in the car, so Olijawan and I took that time to sit together in the back yard and relax. We put some chairs together and sat in the spring sunset. It was one of the first days it was starting to feel warm. We sat out there long enough that I actually got a sunburn. Like who gets a sunburn in April? While we sat out there, I talked to baby and told her "I am ready for you whenever you are, but only you know the perfect time."

We went through the rest of the day as normal, dinner, bath time, brush teeth, bed time. Once Omari was asleep we went to the room and got comfortable in bed to watch a movie. Suddenly at 9:45 I felt a sudden pop, then an explosion of water. I gasped, out of surprise more than anything else. It startled Olijawan and he asked what was wrong, I said "my water just broke." He said "really?!" "Yeah, can you get me a towel?" "I gotta text my boss and tell them I can't come in tomorrow." "Are you fuckin kidding me?! just get me a towel and then you can text your boss."

I'm just sitting in a puddle of amniotic fluid and he's just hyped he gets the day off. Once I got all cleaned up I put on a super cute adult diaper and started laundry while I waited for active labor to start.

At 10:27 I had my first recognizable contraction. I was anxious and excited for things to pick up. From the beginning, the contractions were very sporadic. They weren't very consistent but they picked up intensity quickly. I bounced on my ball for an hour or so and then decided to try to rest before things got more intense.

Resting didn't last long though, the contractions quickly became strong enough I couldn't sleep through them. So I decided to get up and grab my yoga ball and wireless headphones and try to zone out in the dark living room. The contractions would come strong every few minutes for an hour or so and then just stop. I was becoming exhausted and annoyed. Everytime I would get discouraged with the lull in labor I would try to accept it as a moment to rest, but as soon as I would become comfortable enough to sleep, I was hit with another wave of surges.

I was falling asleep on my yoga ball leaned over on the couch in between contractions. I just wanted labor to make up its damn mind. Either come in full force or fuck off and let me sleep. This went on all night.

Once the sun started to come up, I texted my chiropractor and let him know I was in labor and it kept stalling and I thought an adjustment would be helpful. He agreed as long as I promised not to give birth in his office, so we set an appointment for around 10am. We got Omari all packed up and I sat on a puppy pad lined passenger seat and rode very uncomfortably on the 10 minute drive to the chiropractor's office. Thank god I didn't have any contractions in the car.

Once we got there, I checked in, and got adjusted, and almost immediately after, I stood up to leave and had a huge contraction. I just stood there breathing, waiting for it to go away. The receptionist ladies have known us for a long time and are so kind. They just watched with empathetic looks, all I wanted was to crawl back into my birthing hole at home. We got back into the car and took the dreaded ride home. Once we were home, my contractions continued the obnoxious inconsistent pattern. I would walk back and forth in our back yard and they were coming every couple minutes, and as soon as I would sit to rest, they would stop. I was getting discouraged. I couldn't figure out what was going on.

Olijawan was taking care of Omari but we had my dad and step mom on stand by to get him if need be, I really wanted him there, but it just got to a point that I think it was a distraction, and I needed Olijawans help and attention. So I called to have them get him and they came around 1pm. The moment they picked him up, it was like the mental block had been removed and my contraction came full force and never stopped. I immediately went into transition once he left.

I got in the shower for some relief and asked Olijawan to get in with me. It helped briefly. But I just became uncomfortable again. So I got my robe on and went to the living room and leaned over my yoga ball. I leaned and rocked and moaned through each contraction as Olijawan watched and checked on me, he went into the drawer and grabbed my birth affirmations I had printed. He began taping them on the entertainment center in front of me.

He was so calm and quiet. He just followed me around the house whenever I moved and did whatever I asked.

I moved back and forth from the floor, to the yoga ball, to the shower, then the bathtub, and back again. I was to the point where I thought I couldn't do it any more, and I told Olijawan, when I get to the point that I think I can't go any further, remind me, I already am and it's almost done.

I finally ended up in the bedroom. I was laying on the bed trying to focus and relax into the contractions but my body would tense up. I felt like I was losing control and I couldn't stop it. I remember being so exhausted, I looked at Olijawan, and I felt scared, and he just looked at me and said "I trust you, you're okay." I wanted to give up so badly. But it was literally impossible. The only way to make it end was to see it through.

I began feeling the urge to push with my contractions. It gave me something to work for. I was so tired and wanted it to end. I moved from the bed to the floor and rode the contractions. Pushing, as my body told me to. I was so tired I could barely keep my eyes open. I remember thinking, either come out now or just wait till later cause I'm so fuckin tired. I felt inside to see if I could feel her head and I couldn't feel anything at first. I was so discouraged, I started to panic. When would she come? How long would it take?

More contractions came, I pushed with my body, I felt inside again and I felt something hard. My heart leapt with relief. It. Was. Almost. Over.

I was sitting with one leg up and the other bent on the ground leaning back on my hands, but I needed more leverage. So I rocked forward and squatted at the end of our bed. And in one contraction, her head just slipped into place. She moved all the way down and started crowning. And boy when they say "ring of fire" it is no fuckin joke. It burned so bad. I didn't have time to think, or wait, or breath through it. My body bared down and roared. Olijawan sat behind me with his hands underneath me, preparing to catch her. Her head came out and I had a sudden moment of clarity, I asked where my phone was, I wanted pictures, he said "I'm not goin anywhere, I gotta catch her." Before I could even argue, another surge came and she shot out into his hands. She instantly let out a cry to let us know she was breathing and healthy. I sat back and he handed her to me.

I did it. I fuckin did it. All by myself. And it fuckin hurt. But she's here. I sucked her nose out with my mouth, instinctually, to make sure her airways were clear. She was fine, she was breathing fine, she was calm, and warm.

Olijawan helped me onto the bed before I decided I wanted to get in the bath and get some blood off. We went to the bathroom and I sat on the toilet and felt more contractions and pressure, and I knew the placenta had released. I had Olijawan get me a bowl and birthed the placenta into the bowl on the floor.

Me and baby got into an herbal bath and relaxed. I looked at Olijawan and said "I don't wanna do that again. Not for a really long time." We waited to cut or clamp her cord till it was completely white and limp and no longer pulsing. We let Omari help us cut it.

She was born at (or around) 5:20pm, weighing 9lbs 11.5oz and 22in, almost 3lbs heavier than her big brother. 100% natural and at home with no medication. I did tear, only minorly, but I chose to let it heal naturally without stitches, I just rested and kept my legs together to allow the tissue to rejoin.

It was the most invigorating and empowering experience I've ever had. It was so goddamn hard, but I cannot wait to do it again and again. No doctors. No strangers. No bright light, or gloves and IVs. Just mommy and baby and daddy to catch

Olivia Lynch

Dream birth

I was 41 1/2 weeks, so I was so ready to give birth. My other pregnancies were 39 weeks, so I was surprised to carry him for so long. I decided to try every induction method I know, and if I didn't have him by Saturday August 7th, I would take castor oil as a last resort. I tore so badly with my other 2, I was really freaked out by how big this baby was getting! I did all the usual at home things: primrose oil, 5w, long walks, sex, semen, orgasms, nipple stimulation, spicy food, pineapple, magnesium and calcium, curb walking, a long drive on a bumpy road.... on and on.

On August 4th I got acupuncture to induce, and on the 5th I asked my chiropractor to induce me. Well he came the next day, on August 6th! No castor oil! Thank Goddess!

I woke up at 4 am having strong surges. I had about 5 in 30 minutes and I felt the baby corkscrew his way down into my pelvis!!! It was so incredible! So I KNEW it was finally happening! I then woke my husband. We had lots of skin to skin time and made love. The moment his semen hit my cervix, the intensity of the surges doubled. I was so grateful!

My cousin and her husband have been staying in our guest house next door to help on our farm. When our 2 boys woke up, ages 8 and 10, I told them our baby was coming today and sent them next door, as we had arranged, so I could birth in private.

We had a friend who was supposed to act as our doula, but we couldn't get ahold of her, so I called another doula friend and asked her to come and she did. (I'm a doula, and I have a lot of doula friends.) She was such an angel! I'm so glad she was with us. My cousin was also with us, handling all the practical things. She layed out the supplies, filled the tub, fed everyone, brought drinks out, and took photos and videos. Her husband was next door with my kiddos. I feel like I had the most perfect birth team!

I took a shower and then labored outside in the grass for a few hours. Walked around a bit, but I really needed to be on my hands and knees for every surge. My husband checked my cervix and thought I was about 5-6 cm. I felt kind of pushy, so I was thinking I might be farther than that. But it was several more hours till my water broke in the grass and I felt REALLY pushy.

I got in my outdoor clawfoot tub. I could feel that I had a cervical lip. The pain was so sharp. I kept saying I couldn't do it anymore. It was so much more painful than I remember. I hope it's over soon, etc. I was thinking "I'm never doing this again."

I was moaning and growling all day. With my other births I was SO QUIET, but with this one, I tried to hold it in.

At one point, to direct my energy down but I absolutely could not do it. I had watched lots of birthing videos with my sons to prepare them for the birth in case they decided to be present. But we only watched quiet, peaceful births! When my 8 yr old son came over to see me, he got scared because of all my growling and went back next door. It's ok. I had told them both if they choose to be here or not, it's ok with me. Just go by how they feel in the moment.

I had set the goal to wait for FER to do the work for me. I tore both times before because of coached pushing. I had never really felt FER before. I tried holding the lip back and giving some little pushes when I felt the urge, but didn't feel much movement. My doula suggested that I may be resisting a bit. I told her I was feeling fearful about tearing. She said "ok, now we've named the fear and you can release it. Let it go." And that's all I needed to hear. She said to really let go and give it a big push to see if it felt good. So I did and it felt amazing.

I could still feel the water bag bulging, even though my water broke earlier, I had only lost a trickle. So I ripped the bag open and felt my baby's sweet hairy head. It was so motivating. I pushed harder and felt his head slip past my bones and into my vagina. I started to feel slight burning, so I tried to push slow. With one contraction I thought "oh no! I can't stop it now! My body is just pushing on its own!" And his head came out. One surge, 3 pushes. The burning was only slight, so I felt like I probably did not tear. I finally got to experience the Fetal Ejection Reflex!

My husband seemed surprised to see his head! He told me

"sweetie! The head is out!" As if I didn't know! He burst into tears holding our baby's head.

With the next push, I figured his body would slide out like my other boys, but he did not. I had to push SO HARD to get his shoulders out. It was almost as hard as the head. And then his body slid out. He was pretty well tangled in his cord, around his armpits and neck. He had absolutely NO VERNIX at all, and long fingernails. He did not cry. He was purple. I rubbed his back and he started up. I asked our doula to go get the boys and they came really fast. Baby was a bit gurgly, so Papi sucked out his nose and mouth with his mouth.

I stayed in the tub about 10 minutes to try to push the placenta out, but baby was getting cold, so we decided to move inside. As soon as I stood up, I felt it sliding out, so our doula put the bowl under me. The placenta seemed HUGE.

I sat down on the couch to nurse him, and he latched immediately and stayed latched for an hour on each side. 2 hours! Then he finally fell asleep. I took a shower, and went pee. NO BURNING! NO TEARS! We all thought he looked like a really big baby, so we cut his cord at that time and weighed him. 9lbs 2oz! My biggest baby, by far! And 14 inch head. 19 inches long.

Our chiropractor came to the house and gave the baby his first adjustment. When he had his neck adjusted, he spit up a bit of amniotic fluid. Another friend came by to pick up the placenta to encapsulate.

My sweet husband keeps kissing me and thanking me for having his baby. This is his first child. We layed the baby between us in bed and stared at him till we fell asleep. Baby woke a lot to spit and cough up amniotic fluid. When he finally had his first pee and poo in the morning and changed him, he cried a good cry for the first time and I thought it was good because it sounds like it cleared his lungs.

His latch is great! He's a very content baby. Big brothers adore him. I feel fantastic. Barely any blood loss. I had my cousin and best friend take care of my farm and house today. The neighbors heard me give birth outside, so they brought food over. We are so well cared for! And I feel so empowered! We had our absolute dream birth with no complications whatsoever.

Brandi

Jack Henry Dylan

Jan 29 2022 10:05 PM
9.2 lbs

I hit my 40th week of my completely wild pregnancy and expected it to last another 2. I'd packed all my birthing supplies, tinctures, oils and resources into a handy box and awaited the day. I bought double what was recommended by anyone since my second birth, an attended home birth was traumatic. I was so weak, I bled a lot and struggled to bond with my beautiful daughter. I refused to allow that to happen this time. I'd rather be twice prepared than just halfway.

The day the Canadian Freedom Convoy rolled through Ontario, Jan 28 2022, I packed my kids up (my son is 4, daughter 2.5) and drove 3 hours to my sister Josie's house to be able to watch it pass. The three days leading up to the 28th I had constant dull cramps. After the drive I felt stiff, cramping and sore. The mild cramping wasn't unusual because for 3-4 weeks I'd been cramping and uncomfortable on and off. I figured I was due around January 30 so I wasn't surprised or concerned by the cramping.

49

That night after we watched the convoy, around 11pm I wasn't cramping but definitely sore. I felt my waters break at 1am, not a full rupture but in gushes. I thought it was urine because there wasn't a huge amount. I went to the toilet and when I stood I felt more trickle. I sat and peed, stood and felt another trickle. It was tinged pink so I knew it was my water and cervix opening. Since I was visiting my sister, I had nothing packed to wear for padding. She knew something was up and came into the bathroom within moments of my being in there. Thankfully she brought some receiving blankets as pads for me to use. I called my husband Dylan and gave him the heads up that I may be driving home with a third child. He asked that I call if anything progresses as I hadn't had any contractions at this point. I managed to sleep 3am- 7am.

I woke and had mild contractions every 5 minutes so I called Dylan again and he came to me at Josie's house. I focused on relaxing every muscle during the rushes. I'd soften my lips, open and relax my throat, soften and relax my vagina and all the muscles I could.

By the time Dylan got there 3 hours later, the contractions would space out to 10, 20 minutes. Most brought gushes or large amount of mucus/ blood streaked plug. If it wasn't a mucus rush, it was a small rush of waters.

I wanted to be at home. I told my body and baby it was happening at my sister's unless we could hold off for 4 hours. I had no contractions in the 30 minutes it took to pack and load my car, so I saw it as a sign that my body would not bring this baby earth side unless I was having the birth I envisioned at our home. I started wearing the disposable underwear Dylan brought me, as each contraction still brought much mucus or fluid. Dylan took our oldest son home, Josie came with me to relieve me if the contractions returned and our daughters were going with us.

Around 230 we were loaded up, got gas and food and hit the road with Josie and the girls. Dylan would meet us at home. I had a few contractions on the road but nothing unusual for the day. Once we hit my road, at 645 pm I got 2 fairly close together.

Once I got into the house I had quite a few come 2-3 minutes apart and then they spaced from 2 to 5 minutes but increasingly stronger. Dylan and my son got home around 730. They were much stronger by no but no less than 5-6 minutes between them.

By 8, my daughter was ready for bed. I had a quick, hot shower and she joined me. The contractions stopped again while I was focused on her. I had one that signaled it was time to get her to bed. I laid with her til she slept, realizing this would be my last night with her as my youngest baby. After this night, she would be a big sister. I wanted to lay with her all night and pause.

A very strong pressure contraction pushed me out of bed at 8:30. When I got back up, I struggled to find a place to rest, to prepare. I paced between the bathroom and the living room. I tried to put on a movie, settle on the couch but I knew I was further than I realized in labor and that I needed to find my space.

I was drinking OJ straight from the jug by this point because water just wasn't satisfying, and I wanted to keep my blood sugar up. We set my tinctures and birth kit on the coffee table. I took rescue remedy frequently, any time I felt a shiver or feeling of being off.

The two toddlers still awake were playing close by, my son often offered his help with breathing and holding my hand. I was feeling very sensory overloaded when my contractions came by 9pm, I wanted more quiet during them, less commotion. I told my son I needed him to be still when my body was working. He was so in tune and excited for his sibling to come.

I felt an urgency to find my position. I sat on the blankets we had made on the floor, in the front of the wood-stove. That didn't feel good, the contraction was more painful in a sitting position. I moved up and into a half squat, half kneel and the same feeling was there. I settled on my knees, leaning forward on my couch. This felt good.

Around 930, very soon after I settled in a position, I felt the ballooning in my cervix and the baby began to make his descent. We spread the chux pads out as my pants were long gone by this point. We sent the kids to the room to play during the last phase. Dylan chose to step in with them and come out to check on me every few minutes. He knew I was doing what I needed to and he needed to keep the kids from distracting me for the next rushes.

I had my hands pushed on the cushions, I was still on my knees on the floor and my body was pushing upright. I felt him descend, and told my sister to prepare to guide his body to the floor. I had 2-3 contractions that brought him to crowning. I felt the feeling of "I can't do this" creep in, and I just moaned out that I had to get through it. His head came through and I had such a deep tremor run through me of pure adrenaline. I said my sister's name. She said "I've got them" and just patted my hip. I forced myself to pant, to release my teeth from a clench and try to relax. The next surge felt mild, it was all my FER that was pushing him down. I continued to try to pant but I felt like I was tightening in response to the FER so I let myself bear down and growled his head fully out.

I felt the start of a very small tear, similar to a scratch and just panted. I felt a deep pressure in the front of my birth canal. I guess the shoulder in the position change? I felt that I had enough at this point and told her the baby was coming, bore down and he came free.

He came earthside at 10:05. Josie guided him to the towel and I turned to sit. I had a small rush of blood on the pads. I lifted his soft, wet body to my chest and just looked at his face. I felt no fear of bleeding this time. A boy. He looked pale but not white, alert, not limp. I could see he was there, I was in no rush. I sucked his nose twice and only got a few trickles of fluid so I left him to do the work. He began to cry within moments and his skin turned a perfect pink. I drank OJ and took rescue remedy. I had no tremors, shakes or feelings of lightheadedness.

I rubbed his back gently. My uterus felt very tight, not quite a contraction. He settled and nursed well, content and alert. I felt the urge to release the placenta but I wasn't sure if it was a second baby. I pressed down on my belly and felt the rigid lines of a form, I handed the baby to my sister and crouched and blew into my fist. I felt the birth of the placenta and let it fall to the pad beneath me. I knew I would not eat this one. This birth was so beautiful and my body felt so strong that I knew I would not need the placenta and what it offered me from my last birth.

I moved onto the couch on a pad and felt small trickles of blood but I knew I would not hemorrhage. At 10:30 my son, 4 years old, had the honour of cutting the cord, with daddy's help. He was so proud to bear witness to his brother's entrance.

This was the most amazing experience. Pure, primal and real. Redemptive. Honouring. And he is so worthy of it all.

Kayla

Summer Solstice baby

I welcomed my baby, Maya Savannah, at 3:03am on June 21st, the summer solstice. Her birth was my third vaginal, but first homebirth and first unassisted. She was born at 42 weeks and 3 days gestation.

I had my dream birth: outside on our screened lanai, in a warm pool, in the middle of the night. There were twinkle lights and candles and the sounds of nature all around. My other children were sleeping peacefully in their rooms. I had no need for outside help, just my husband's calm support. I listened to my body and caught my baby by myself. It was magic and bliss.

At 12 weeks pregnant I had one non-medical ultrasound, to see the baby and confirm the heartbeat. From then on I chose an intuition-lead pregnancy. Despite knowing less information, I felt so in tune with my body. Whenever I had any worries or doubts the baby would instantly kick. It seemed as if she knew exactly what I was thinking, and gave me the reassurance that I needed. It was so empowering to rely only on my own knowledge and connection with my baby, rather than a medical provider's set of generic rules.

However, the last week of pregnancy was rough for my body and mind. I had contractions starting and stopping all day, every day, and becoming more intense each time. I had not experienced this with my previous labors. Going past my estimated due date by over two weeks made this my longest pregnancy as well. I knew third babies were called "wild cards" by the midwife community, but I hadn't expected this. I desperately tried to keep my sanity, and faith in the process, during those days.

I had strong inconsistent contractions all day on the 20th, which was becoming my new normal. Then after dinner, around 7pm, they became consistent. I never timed them because being in and out of labor for so long, it just didn't seem important anymore. By the time my two toddlers were in bed at 9pm I needed to get quiet and breathe through them. By 11pm I was making noise and knew this was probably going to be the real thing.

I went outside on the lanai to turn on the lights and candles, and set everything up. The weather was warm, but not too warm. As contractions continued to intensify I repeated mantras to myself that felt good in the moment. "Thank you cervix for softening and allowing my baby to come down," as I said this one I envisioned my cervix easily opening for the baby to descend. When things got tough I thought, "I can do anything for one minute." Also, I reminded myself, "the peak of a contraction only lasts 20 to 30 seconds."

The affirmations helped me relax into the waves of intensity instead of fighting them. Yet, by 1am I was needing more relief. I wanted the birth pool filled. My husband, Kenny, started to get it ready but found out he couldn't fit the hose adapter on any of our sinks. He eventually ran the hose through the lanai window, into our bathroom, and duct taped it to where the shower head connects. It worked well enough to get the pool filled with hot water, and I was so thankful.

When the pool filled enough to submerge myself, I got in and it felt great. I had Kenny bring me a bowl of ice water and wash cloths. I soaked the cloths in the cold water, and then placed them on my head and neck. It was a nice contrast to the warm water and air around me. I huffed on a dry wash cloth with a few drops of lavender essential oil on it. This helped me remember to breathe deeply and relax. I did some comb squeezes as well, and they were a nice distraction for a bit.

As contractions grew stronger, I no longer wanted any of the extra things. I felt I needed all of my energy to go towards birthing. I asked Kenny to turn off the twinkle lights because they were starting to bother me. I wanted darkness and solitude. I asked him to wait inside. He did not want to leave me, but I reassured him that I would yell for him when it was time. I wanted to be alone with the stars and the songs of the crickets.

Nothing but the sounds of the night and my own roars filled the air. I shouted into the dark and as I did, suddenly I did not feel alone anymore. I felt surrounded by spirits, ancestors, and other birthing women from the past. It felt as if they gathered around me in support. I could feel their presence as they held me, encouraged me, and showed me my own strength. They reminded me that this is what I was made to do, and I felt no fear.

Kenny came to add boiling water to the pool, to keep the temperature up. He then stayed with me outside. Loud, deep, primal sounds were coming from me. The intensity was reaching it's peak and I felt the urge to push. In my two previous labors I didn't feel like pushing until after my water had broken. I hadn't felt my water break just yet, so I was surprised I wanted to push. I blindly gave over to the urge because it felt so satisfying.

After a little while I reached down and slipped my finger inside to find the baby's head was only a couple of inches away! This gave me the motivation to keep pushing. I was on my knees, my buttocks sitting on my popped heels. I kept my fingers down at the opening. I had never done this before, as I had never had this kind of privacy and control, to see what really felt good to me. Keeping my hand there helped me to connect to my body and decreased the pain.

I had no idea of time, but some had passed and then the baby's head was at the entrance. It was still in the amniotic sac. Just then my body took over pushing. I had never experienced FER (fetal eject reflex) before, but I knew this was it. I was no longer roaring, I was silent. I closed my eyes and tried to relax as the baby made her way down.

I felt the bag of waters still around her head, but once it was pushed all the way out, the bag broke. For a brief moment time stood still. I remember touching her ears, how cute and little they felt. I told Kenny to take his phone out and record it. We had been so in the moment, we both forgot about getting a birth video. He caught just the end of it on camera, because with the next involuntary push her entire body came flying out.

I caught her and brought her to my chest. She did not cry right away, but she was pink. I brought my mouth to her face to suction any fluid. I didn't feel she needed it, but I tried once more before bringing her to my chest, and rubbing her back. She then cried and I was elated. I felt so alive. Saying to my baby, "Hello!" "You're perfect!" And to my husband I said, "Oh my God, that was incredible!" I don't have enough words to describe the feeling, but it lasted with me for weeks after birth. It was like a surreal, unimaginable high.

Some more moments had passed as I soaked in the glory of our new baby and her sweet little cry. Then I looked to Kenny and said, "We still don't know what we have!" I lifted her up and announced, "It's a girl!" This was my first pregnancy where we didn't know the gender prior to birth. We already had a boy and a girl, and wanted a surprise this time. My whole pregnancy I went back and forth between thinking it was a girl or boy. Then the last week, I felt more and more that it was a girl. Now I couldn't stop smiling.

I wanted to get out of the pool and go to my bedroom to nurse and deliver the placenta. There was hardly any blood in the pool, but as I stood up two big chunks came out. What I first thought was my placenta, turned out to be a couple of large clots. This had never happened to me before and was a little shocking. Kenny grabbed the angelica for me to put under my tongue, just in case.

I had never given birth to my placenta by myself, so I was curious how it would go. The birth center where my other children were born in, forced it out at 20 to 30 minutes post birth. I never liked the experience, and knew I wanted to give it patience this time. I laid in bed, skin to skin with my baby. I nursed her and took the angelica tincture. After an hour or so I felt the urge to push. I got out of the bed, asked Kenny to put the placenta bowl on the floor, and handed him the baby. I squatted over it, pushing once, while giving the cord a little traction with my fingers, and out it flopped! In the end it was so simple. It made me wonder why so many birth attendants feel the need to medically manage this stage of labor.

I did not pass any more clots and had minimal bleeding. I checked for tears and had none. My entire vulva felt perfectly fine right after. It didn't sting when I used the bathroom. I didn't need the peri bottle or padsicles I had prepared. The baby looked great, and was latching and nursing wonderfully. I sat on the floor by the bed on some puppy pads and ate the dates I asked Kenny to get from the fridge. I felt cloaked in the purest happiness, with my new baby asleep in my arms.

As I bathed in the bliss of my dream birth coming to fruition, Kenny asked what we should name her. We hadn't chosen a name just yet, but we had a few that we had discussed. I knew I wanted it to be Maya Savannah right away, but I answered, "I don't know, what do you think?"

He said, "I think she looks like a Maya Savannah," and my heart smiled as I responded, "Oh good, me too." It felt so meant to be.

Next, Kenny asked if we should burn the cord. I had bought a large pillar beeswax candle to burn it with. I had gotten the idea from someone in an online birth group. They stated that they kept the candle, and lit it each year on the baby's birthday. I loved the ceremonial aspect and decided this was how I wanted it done. So Kenny took over the burning of the cord while I held Maya. It took about 10 minutes or so and then he tied the remaining cord in a knot.

I stayed naked and skin to skin with Maya for a while. Eventually, we did her height measurement and weight. I guessed she was 7lbs 6 oz and Kenny guessed 7lbs 8oz. She ended up being only 7 lbs 3 oz, and was 20.5 inches long. She was not my biggest baby, but also not my smallest.

At 8am our 3 year old son and 2 year old daughter woke up and met their newest sibling. It seemed to be a shock to them, since they had both slept through the entire labor. Now Maya is 3 months old and they both love her endlessly. We all do. She has the most calm and happy demeanor. She is such a beautiful addition to our family, and we feel so lucky to have her with us.

I want to thank Heather Baker and her book, "Homebirth on Your Own Terms" for teaching me so much and giving me the confidence to create my dream birth. I wish all women had access to this kind of information and felt confident birthing outside of the medical system. There is no better feeling than giving birth in your power, and bringing life into the world peacefully at home.

Erin Elliott

Full control this time

At 13 weeks pregnant I heard the term free birth for the first time. By 27 weeks I had made my decision that I was going to free birth. At the time the hospital was only allowing one birth support partner and you had to wear a mask. I had already had one very traumatic hospital birth where I had five birth partners, my mum, two friends, my husband and my step daughter, Madison there, who was 18 at the time.

For my second birth I intended to have my husband and both my step daughters there. While I love my husband, I craved the feminine energy around me in this sacred transition. I wanted my son's older sisters welcoming him into the world and holding me in that space. This was only going to be possible outside of the system. I hired a wonderful birthkeeper who radiated warmth and love and read a book she had loaned me - Home Birth On Your Own Terms by Heather Baker!

I had had a late night the night before I went into labour. I was struggling to sleep and uncomfortable at 40+ 5. My 3 year old had woken us at 4am, cranky and came into our bed. At 5 am I woke up feeling some contractions. Having had a fake labour start a few days earlier, I wasn't sold that this was it but regardless, I took the chance to rest and laid in bed just breathing through each gentle contraction. Around 7 am my husband Jay and Max, my 3 year old started to wake up. I said to Jay I've been having pains for the last two hours. I think that I might be going into labour. He didn't believe me as a week beforehand I had also thought the same thing.

Around 9am, he brought me a coffee and some breakfast and as I got up the contractions started to get a little stronger. I bounced on the ball a while, then as the pain became stronger I started to take some things down to our granny flat where I had set up my birthing space. As each contraction came I said
"surrender" …"embrace" and danced through these waves

The surges became stronger and stronger, I started to get a little louder each time, Max gave me lots of cuddles and Jay rubbed my back every time I had a contraction as I walked around the house and yard. I decided it was time to call the girls and my birthkeeper to let them know I thought things were starting. But during the few minutes on the phone to my birthkeeper I had two contractions very close together. I couldn't speak through them so she decided to head over. I put high frequency music on and fully immersed in the experience.

Now everything was fully in place. I moved into the yard and sat on my ball in the beautiful sunshine. It rained for days around the labour so it was nice to sit in the sun and envision the sun cleansing me. Everything was set. I'd done all the hard work, the learning and unlearning, and I knew it was time to get into the zone.

I ate some snacks and had some coconut water while my younger step daughter, Madison arrived. Moments later, so did my birth keeper, Trish. I felt a big shift and pains. Their timing was perfect. Trish held a heat pack on my back while Maddie rubbed my back. We spent some time soaking in the sun listening to soft music and breathing through the surges. I'm not sure how long passed but it started to get a lot stronger and Trish asked if I wanted to try the bath for pain relief. It was HEAVEN.

At this point I was very much in my own world. It felt like a lifetime but so fast at the same time. I remember looking up at the walls where I had hung birth affirmation cards. I remember every now and again, one would catch my eye right at the right time, reminding me how strong I was and why I was here.

I was very quiet other than moaning through the surges, I remember eating fairly frequently and Trish giving me sips of coconut water . Once I was in the bath for a while, Jay came down to the flat and everyone else left. He sat with me and we shared a few kisses and cuddles over the side of the pool. The contractions got stronger.

Kaitlyn arrived and the four of them took turns being with Max outside in the yard or being with me. Max came into the flat and saw that we had a pool. He was so excited that he completely stripped down and jumped in with me. It was nice that he had a few splashes. He really just wanted to swim, so Jay set him up his own pool in the yard where I could actually see it from the window. But Max really wanted to swim in the pool in the flat, so we decided to call Jay's Mum, Yvonne, so he could go stay at home with her. She could keep him distracted at the main house.

I really don't know how long went by, a few hours maybe, then felt the shift where the pain was getting a lot stronger. Everyone just kept reminding me of my affirmations and rubbing my back. All of a sudden from the back of my brain I remembered that some women get a dark line above their tailbone when their cervix had dilated. I also remember reading that in transition is when you feel the most amount of doubt... I started to wonder if I had even dilated. I thought, I can't do this anymore. I was in so much pain, the feelings I had at my first birth while in the hospital, came rushing back. Then I realised, this rush of self doubt... I was transitioning! My baby was so close. I asked Maddie if I had a line on my bum. She had a look and she said "oh yes you do!" I knew right then and there that my body had done all of the work. I trusted it and the Universe and it provided for me.

I relaxed deeper. I remember the pain getting really strong and then I vomited. After that, I felt really tired so I laid on the side of the pool for a bit. I actually fell asleep. Kati was holding a pillow for me in between little sleeps. After some large contractions, I said I think I'm nearly ready to push. I can hear the doubt in Jay's voice when he said, "Are you sure?" Trish said "You know your body darling. You go and get your boy."

After a few deep breaths, I felt restless and I needed to change my positions. I moved my leg up and didn't like it so I moved to a squatting position. I felt the most intense shift in my body. Vance moved down, it was time. Jay was pushing hard on my back to relieve pain and I knew he was going to be there to catch our son but I asked him to be sure, because he had not really done any reading with me. I wasn't sure if he felt confident, but he was.

I pushed and I could feel EVERYTHING. It was incredible to feel it this time. I had no more doubts because I was so in tune with what was happening. It felt so natural and right. I thought his head was out, I reached down and realised I had a way to go but he was there. "It's gonna happen Jem, he's right there," Jay said. I heard Maddie say "he's coming Jem" while Trish poured warm water over my body and Kati rubbed my face and hair with a cool face washer

The way everyone held space and love for me gave me so much strength. Jay had been so hesitant with my plans I could hear how much he believed in me in that moment… I had spent time thinking I wouldn't get the support team I wanted and here I was… the room felt so full of love. Jay instinctively moved his hands to catch Vance. It took a few pushes to get his whole body out.

Jay waited till he was all the way out and caught him bringing him up to my chest. He let out a little cough and a cry by the time he had come to my chest. All of the little fears I had when I made the choice to birth unassisted were gone, done. He was here. He was safe. I protected my body, my space, my baby.

My sweet boy was beyond perfect and ready for milk, so I made my way out of the pool and into the bed in the flat. With lovey warm blankets we snuggled and fed while we all excitedly talked about what an incredible experience we just had together.

My placenta took about an hour to come. I used a placenta release tincture and Vance was happy at the breast. I was kind of antsy to get it out because I wanted Max to come meet Vance. It was so amazing having it come naturally… something I was so upset about in my first birth. It always stuck with me. Having full control of it this time felt so right and so natural. By the time it came out, the whole chord was white. Maddie and Kati tied the cord with a beautiful cotton tie my sister had made and they cut the cord. Yvonne and Max came down and as a family and we proudly beamed together on the beautiful birth that had just taken place. Trish made sure I was drinking some tea and eating some food. After a few hours we made our way inside, showered in my own shower and went into my own bed with our new little baby.

Jemma

Liberating me

Words can't even describe how amazing birth was. She was liberating. Fierce and so incredibly empowering. Forcing me to go within, trust my body and intuition. Tune in with my baby and remove all external paradigms of what's known as "the birth system."

Arnhem-Sol was teaching us patience. Born at 41+1 she made such a quick entrance into the world. From the first sign of contractions around 7-7:30pm to being birthed at 12:25am. I was in a little denial and couldn't process the 2.5 minute apart contractions that all of a sudden hit me.

We slowly started setting up the birth equipment and let our doula know that something was starting. Cooked dinner, cleaned up and laughed in between. Completely underestimating that we'd be holding our baby within a few short hours.

Our doula Kayla arrived and worked her magic. Things were becoming more intense and so I hopped in the pool which was amazing. I hated being on land. I honestly had no concept of time. Before I knew it I was in the midst of transition having an inner dialogue with myself about needing to poop and that I should probably take my undies off.

Within a matter of minutes I could feel her little head of hair. I calmly asked my partner if he wanted to catch his baby. I don't think he quite knew how close we were. After asking him again he hopped in the pool and she ejected out. It felt like she was being pulled out (she wasn't) and at the time I didn't realise that FER was happening.

Arnhem-Sol was so peaceful just observing us before letting out a cry. I instinctively sucked mucous out but there wasn't much at all. Nor was there much blood in the pool. After finding out her gender and soaking it all in, we then went on to birth the placenta. It took a few hours and we utilized a few after birth tinctures to help aid the process. We gently thanked the placenta.

Bubba and dad had skin to skin whilst I had a shower. Around 4am we went on to have the most beautiful cord burning ceremony. Dad made the most lovely cord burning box to use. We spoke to Arnhem-Sol and explained the transition.

Kayla was so amazing, she was so present but it didn't feel like she was there. She truly held space for us through it all.

Her big brother came home at 12pm and was totally smitten. We organized a cake for her 1 day old birthday and soaked in life as a family of four.

Tiana

Birth story of Bodhi

7am: I woke up Friday morning with my sweet Saoirse in my arms. She often comes up from sleeping with her dad, to coming up to my bed to snuggle me early in the morning. We generally all sleep together because we have our full and king bed flush with the ground but by the end of my pregnancy we stacked the full on top of the king for the last couple weeks for my comfortability. We did our usual wonder around the room routine.

9am: She found a bottle of prenatal pills that she ended up playing with. I walked over to pick them up and did a deep squat. Right as I went down, I felt this huge gush of water and thought it was weird because it was way more liquid than anytime I've ever accidentally peed my pants. My husband woke up because of the sound in my voice that just didn't seem right. This being my 5th pregnancy I've never experienced my water breaking before so I wasn't sure what to expect or if it was even my water that broke in the first place. It just kept coming out with every movement I made. That was my first indication that it could be the real thing.

I went and sat on the toilet and just waited a couple

minutes to see if maybe it was just pee and make sure my bladder was empty. I stood up and more liquid proceeded to come out. My mind kind of went blank. I started to cry! I realized today might be the day I get to meet my baby! I texted my sister and told her I thought my water may have broken and started to cry a little harder coming to the realization that she wouldn't be here while I was in labor. I released all of the expectations I had hoped for in that moment.

In my pregnancy I really tried to focus on what my dream birth looked like to me. It was so hard to let that dream die and just be present in the moment. I've been using FAM for birth control for over 5 years so when guessing my due date, I calculated it to be 9/25/21. Who knew I'd actually have my baby on my due date?! NOT ME! I've never had a baby so close to my "due date." I expected I'd have an October baby at best. My mind just kept repeating, "I thought I had more time!" Although I was partly still in denial…

I thought it would be a good idea to try and catch some of the water in a jar so I could examine it. As soon as I did that my observation and mind came together. I concluded this was in fact the real deal. The water was tinted a bit yellow with lots of white flakes(vernix) in it. My husband was so comforting and so chill! Everything after that seemed to go in slow motion. I remember texting my photographer that my waters had broken but I wasn't having any waves and I would let her know of an update as soon as things started moving along.

11am: I bounced on my birthing ball and walked around my bedroom for a little while. I let my other kids know today might be the day that their new sibling would be coming!

12pm: I suddenly felt really tired and thought I should lay down as it could end up being a super long day/night. I slept on and off for about 2 hours with some waves in between. Nothing too crazy and they were really inconsistent. I would say maybe 10-20 mins apart.

3pm: I decided to get up and have a snack. Then Benito and I went for a walk in the neighborhood. Waves were still coming but still far apart. When we got back to the house I used the bathroom and noticed my mucus plug was coming out. Not much more water coming out at this point. Baby felt super low too.

5pm: Waves we're coming 10-6 mins apart at this point. I mostly stayed in my room since it's my safe place. I texted the photographer with an update. I knew things could pick up pretty quickly at this point and she lives about 1.5 hours from me. She quickly replied she was on her way.

7pm: Things still seemed to be going in slow motion. Waves were maybe 6-4 mins apart at this time. I asked Benito to fill the tub in case things changed quickly.

9pm: Once the pool was filled, I asked Benito to go on another walk with me. This really helped move things along again! The waves started to become more intense and I'd have to stop to get through them. It was a good sign and

I was starting to get excited for what was to come! That part was really surprising to me because for the last couple of weeks before going into labor I was for some reason nervous about the fears that may come up.

10pm: We came back home, made sure the kids had dinner and then went right back upstairs to my birthing cave. I really wanted to get in the water. It was actually kinda chilly outside when we were walking so the warm water sounded nice!

This is where the time gets kinda iffy for me. Once I was in the tub waves started to come about every 2 minutes or so. Lasting only about 30 seconds. They were bearable but I did need to moan and breathe through them. Trying to remember my 4 counts of breath in and 6 counts out really helped in those moments. I couldn't really vocalize but I remember Saoirse being really cute with our photographer. She kept trying to sit on her lap. She was so interested in the camera flash. It was really cute and a bit of a distraction which I really think I needed at that point. She'd walk over to the tub, look in and just walk away. Soon after that things got super intense.

I remember trying to feel inside to see if I could feel baby's head yet. I could but it was still pretty high up. The waves seemed like so much pressure at this point. I never experienced it like this before and without the cushion of the water bag around the baby, it felt like I could feel everything even more intensely. I could hear it in my voice because I was really vocal at this time and started to feel tense. It was harder to breathe through the waves and I found myself trying to open my throat to get loud and roar through them. When I go back to check the time stamp on some of the video, I found it was around 12am when this started to happen.

With every wave I could feel baby moving down, down, down. Once baby's head was past my pelvic bone I really started to feel some pain. Between waves I would feel where baby's head was and with each wave I started to feel super pushy. I started to push and it almost felt like relief but still painful. I remember looking at my husband in the eyes a couple times not being able to vocalize that I was in so much pain! I was going through this intense portal and it felt like I wasn't even really there. I started to cry while I was pushing with each wave. It felt like they were lasting forever without any breaks in between. I just wanted some relief or for things to slow down. That was silly because of course I was about to push the head out.

I could feel the head almost ready to push through my Yoni. It was only 2 surges before the head started to stretch it. I really tried to blow instead of push at this point. That felt kind of good but still really intense! Two more waves and baby's head was out. I told Benito he might need to catch from behind because I was just so unsure of what was happening or where baby was going to go. It really just felt like I was in another world and wanted to make sure someone caught the baby.

I was on my knees up until the head came out and then got into a runners position for the next surge as I knew baby may have a better chance of floating up towards me

75

and into my arms rather than float up behind me. The next wave came quickly and I felt baby turn. The shoulders were out and the rest of baby was still inside but came out pretty quickly after.

12:51am: The baby floated right up to me. I grabbed him and noticed how much vernix he had! That was also new to me. None of my other babes had any left on them when they were born. This baby had so much and it was so thick! I took some and rubbed it all over my chest. I talked to baby and just waited for that sweet little cry. It only took maybe 30 seconds. It was so beautiful and so intense! I cried and remember just saying "we did it baby! We did it! That was so crazy, I can't believe we did that!" It felt so good for it to just be over and finally have my baby in my arms.

I asked my son Lukas to check and see if it was a boy or a girl. I spread open baby's legs and I immediately noticed baby had balls! I was so thrilled to have another son. I kind of had this intuition that it was a boy and was just so happy he was here. I waited it out in the tub for maybe 10 minutes but could tell the placenta was ready to be born. Benito helped me out and I just kneeled on the floor with the baby and gave a little push and it slid right out. The sack seemed a bit stuck so Benito had to help with that part as I only had 1 hand and he had to grab it from behind. Easy peasy.

I got in bed with baby and all my other kids and we just marveled at how amazing this new baby boy was. He latched right away and had great suction! It kind of caught me off guard. I was just so happy! Benito grabbed me a snack and some more water. He started to clean up a bit until I was ready to do the cord burning. We waited until around 3:30am to burn the cord. All the kids were asleep at this point except for Nysha so he got to help. Once the placenta and cord were detached, Benito made some prints on canvas with it.

Nysha went to bed and Benito and I just snuggled our new baby. We all went to sleep together around 5am. This birth was simple and beautiful and holy. It was hard work and I really had to work through some pain towards the end but it was of course worth it! After the first freebirth I had, I thought I knew what to expect but I was totally wrong. I'm so grateful for this experience and the story I get to tell. Not everything went as planned but in all honesty, it was just as perfect as the first time. I am forever grateful.

Side Note: I do want to mention that the next morning when I went to the bathroom I noticed a burning sensation. When I checked with my hand mirror it appeared I had torn a small bit. I took some nice baths with Epsom salts and herbs. It healed itself within a week.

Bodhi Beren Palomino
9lbs 4oz
20 inches
12:51 am
9/25/2021

Tiffany

The Family Birth of Azalea Tierra, Our 10th Baby

This is the home birth story of our tenth baby. But first a little of our backstory. All 10 of our babies were born at home unassisted with just myself, my husband and family. Each one of my births has been different, yet all of them beautifully unhindered, empowering, and peaceful.

Some people may assume that my births must be easy, or that I just somehow got 'lucky' that nothing went wrong, and some have even said that I must be some kind of anomaly. I assure you that I am not. My births have not all been easy, and I have experienced many situations that would likely have been labeled as 'complications' in another setting, but as I have learned, most of these were really just variations of normal. I have had such a wide variety of labor and birth experiences, including water births and 'land' births, a long exhausting 36 hour labor with 2 nights of no sleep, as well as a precipitous labor and birth under 2.5 hours, a baby born with an unusually short cord that needed resuscitation, and babies born with the cord wrapped around their neck, birth with meconium, a retained placenta for over 5 hours after birth, and even a crazy unexpected BREECH birth in the front seat of the car!

Each of my 9 previous births challenged me in new ways, each testing my patience and belief in myself. Each birth seemed to push the boundaries in one way or another, yet ultimately deepened my trust in my own intuition and nature's divine wisdom. But, with SO many different birth experiences I really wasn't sure what to expect next with baby number 10. If I've learned to expect anything it's to expect the unexpected. Every birth is different. Each baby's journey is unique to them. Each birth has taught me something new. And so I wondered, what unique situation was going to come my way this time?
Well, this is her story…

My estimated due date of September 20th happened to fall on the full harvest moon, right before the fall equinox. I've learned that due dates don't mean much, as I have gone into labor a month earlier than expected as well as nearly a month 'late'. So, I was actually expecting baby to arrive basically anytime in September or October. But 5 days before that 40-week mark, I felt a definite shift in my hormones that told me the birth was drawing near. I was suddenly feeling extra emotional and also noticed an increase in pressure in my pelvis. I felt heavy and achy, my feet were swollen and sore and I was SO ready to be done being pregnant… yet at the same time I was having anxiety at the thought of labor starting!

My husband Roy happened to be in an extended water fast that he felt was necessary for him to continue, but as

I saw his condition declining I was becoming increasingly concerned both for his well-being and for his ability to support me during labor and birth. My husband caught all of our babies and was always my number one support person. After more than 30 days on only water he was getting weak and began vomiting bile. I begged him to end the fast. I did NOT want to go into labor with him like this! He insisted that he would be fine but he did not look well and worrying about him was causing me to feel so much nervous, negative energy.

The upcoming birth felt like this wall of fire I was facing, knowing I had no choice but to go through it! The only way out was through. I've done this 9 times already and my last few births were quick and smooth. Why was I feeling so much anxiety and fear? I didn't know what to do. I cried. I did some EFT work (emotional freedom technique/tapping) and felt better about the birth but still worried about my husband.

Finally on the night of the due date he agreed to end his fast earlier than he planned. I brought him food and he started regaining his strength and feeling better immediately. I stood outside for a moment in the cool night air and stared up at the full moon feeling a shift in the energy. As we settled into bed that night around midnight I cuddled up to my husband and let out a big sigh of relief. I felt as if a huge weight had been lifted and a feeling of peace fell over me as I drifted off to sleep.

At 4 am I was awakened from a dream by a sensation of warm fluid coming out of me and I immediately thought,

"Did my water just break?" I got out of bed and went to the bathroom. After I went pee, I sat for a moment feeling a little sleepy and confused. Did my water really break or was that just a dream? I stood up and more amniotic fluid trickled out. Yep, my water had definitely broken! I put on a pad and crawled back in bed. I told Roy that my water broke. I was excited but I decided I should get some more sleep while I can since I wasn't in labor yet.

While I was sleeping I felt a couple of contractions that were just strong enough that I was aware of them but slept until about 7:30 am. When I got up I was excited to tell the kids that Daddy broke his water fast AND my water broke! Kind of a funny coincidence? The wording yes, but the timing, probably not. I think perhaps baby was ready but my body had been holding off until I felt conditions were right. It was the 21st of September, the fall equinox. It felt so symbolic that so many things were shifting at once. The end of summer, the end of his fast, the end of my pregnancy, the end of this phase of my life and the beginning of the next phase with a new little member in our family. "Looks like today is Baby Day!" I told them. The kids were excited. Roy put on the very appropriate song "The 21st of September" and everyone went into celebration mode!

I didn't have any contractions for the first hour after getting up. I messaged my Mom, my sister Cierra and good friend Pia that I had invited to be there for the birth. I let them all know that my water had broken but that I wasn't in labor yet. My water had only broken before labor one other time (with baby #5) and it took about 12 hours for labor to start. I thought maybe it would follow a similar timeline so I said I would keep them posted. I was thankful that labor didn't start right away as it gave me a little more time to prepare. My waters continued leaking and I had irregular contractions throughout the day as I cleaned up the house, showered, got birth supplies ready, took a 9-month belly picture, and read some children's home birth books with my kids.

At about 5pm I lost the cervical plug. It was blood streaked so I figured there was probably some dilation going on but didn't feel the need to check dilation. My guess was that labor would probably pick up after dark and that the baby would be born that night. Seemed likely since ALL of my other babies were born between sunset and sunrise. This was one thing all my births had in common. So that evening I told my doula/friend Pia, my sister Cierra, and my Mom that they should probably come over even though I wasn't in active labor yet. I was worried that once labor started that it might go so fast they wouldn't have time to get there. (My last birth was less than 2 hours from when I realized I was in labor to feeling like the baby was going to fall out! We live an hour and a half away from town and it all happened so fast I wasn't able to get in the birth pool and those that I invited didn't make it there in time.) I was hoping that my labor wouldn't be as fast as last time but I also knew it *could* go even faster. The trend with my last few births was that labor was getting shorter and shorter. 'Was this one going to go even faster?', I wondered. It's hard not to form expectations based on past experiences. But, just like always… I was in for some surprises.

My two youngest little girls, Safire, 2, almost 3 and Aria - 4.5 years, were anxiously awaiting their new sibling's arrival and they wanted to be there for the birth. But after waiting all day they were getting impatient. Aria said "When is the baby going to come out? I've been waiting SOOOO long!" They were getting grumpy and I figured I might be getting them up in the middle of the night for the birth so I decided to put them to bed. She didn't want to go to bed and said "I want the baby to come out RIGHT NOW!" Haha! I explained that the baby will come out when it's ready. Maybe it will be tonight! I lay down with them until they fell asleep.

My friend Pia and her daughter Cora, my sister Cierra and my Mom and Dad all arrived. We visited, timed contractions for a while, and my sister gave me a nice foot massage using some clary sage oil that I got because it's said to stimulate or increase contractions. She even tried some pressure points I read about. I enjoyed the company. We sat around the living room talking and laughing while having contractions. Laughing seemed to bring on contractions, and the contractions and laughing caused my water to gush which made me laugh even more! It felt quite comical. But contractions were still random and by about midnight I was getting tired. So we decided to get some rest and everyone turned in for the night. I told them I would wake them if anything started happening. I felt a little disappointed that labor hadn't started yet but also grateful to get some sleep.

When I woke, I was somewhat surprised that it was morning already and everything was still the same. I remember being woken briefly by a few contractions in the night but for the most part slept well. The little ones and I listened to the baby's heartbeat with the doppler and then went into the kitchen to make some tea as everyone started getting up. We decided to take a walk down the road to my in-law's house to update them that everything was the same, - water still leaking, still having contractions but - still waiting on baby. The weather was nice and I took my sandals off to feel my bare feet on the earth. I knew intuitively that all was well. As we walked down the dirt road we joked about how I had said that I hoped my labor wouldn't be as fast as the last one, so now I get an extra long, drawn out, slow labor! I guess that's why they say "Be careful what you wish for!" Haha

Around noon everyone began leaving and I said I would call if anything changes. We sat down to watch a movie and Cierra stayed and gave me another foot massage and pedicure which was so nice! After she left, I took a little nap. All throughout the day contractions continued irregularly, but I was gradually leaking less amniotic fluid. By evening it seemed that the amniotic sac must be sealing back up! I was starting to wonder if I was just going to continue being pregnant for another week or more! And my analytical mind was starting to question, What was taking so long? Was something wrong? Maybe the baby wasn't in a good position? Was there another reason my body was holding back? Should I be doing something to speed things up? But when I searched inward my intuition told me I need NOT try to speed things up. Baby was fine, heartbeat and movement were normal.

I was drinking lots of water to replace lost fluid. Even though it felt like things were moving SO slowly, I knew that I just needed to surrender to the unpredictability of the process and trust that it will unfold just how it needs to. This was just another variation of normal for me to experience. Every baby seems to test my level of trust by giving me another 'outside the box' situation or challenge to overcome. In this case, I didn't need to *do* anything other than trust, relax, rest and keep my body hydrated and nourished through this long early labor.

I went to bed somewhat early, in case active labor kicked in that night. I was still expecting my baby to be born during the night/early morning like all the others. But instead, once again, I slept. I slept pretty good despite being woken briefly a few times throughout the night by some strong contractions. Everything was the same, except that the water wasn't leaking anymore! I lay there in bed between my two littles with my great big belly in the middle wondering how much longer I was going to be pregnant. In any case, in the big picture I knew I wouldn't be pregnant too much longer! And despite being uncomfortable, I knew I would miss my big baby belly and feeling all those sweet little hiccups, kicks and turns.

It had been over 48 hours since my water broke and I was still waiting for labor to begin. But I realized that this early labor was STILL part of the labor process, and not any less important than any other part. It was just so interesting how different each labor can look and how different each stage of labor can be. This slow labor spanning the past two days was peaceful. It was such a blessing really, to be home, surrounded by family and friends who support and trust me. There was no stress, no rush, no interventions, no one pushing their fears on me. I was grateful and I knew that this labor and birth were unfolding just as they were meant to. I was ok with however long it took.

I began my day as usual, deciding that I would just continue working on the projects on my to do list. I thought, 'Maybe I will get to finish my bathroom after all!' Contractions continued the same as before anywhere from 10 to 30 or even 40 minutes apart and some stronger than others. My oldest daughter left for work. I was a little nervous for her to go but I told her I would call if anything changed.

As I was moving about in the kitchen making tea and what not, I began to notice the contractions getting stronger so I kept my phone with me so I could time them. From 10 am to 10:30 they had become regular, about 12 to 13 minutes apart and getting stronger. By 11 am they were coming every 10 minutes and I was starting to have to stop and breathe through them. I told Roy and the kids "I think labor is starting." and I messaged Pia, Cierra and my Mom and told them contractions were starting to get regular and I might be calling them to come soon. I didn't want to get too excited. I guess I was still in denial that I was really FINALLY in active labor! But just as soon as I had texted everyone that labor "might" be starting, the contractions changed from every 10 minutes to only 4 or 5 minutes apart. I knew then that it was definitely labor and getting intense. I told my kids to call Serina and tell her she better come home now. She had just barely arrived at work which was nearly an hour and a half away! I messaged everyone that they should come now. I was feeling a little anxious since labor had picked up in intensity so quickly and I was worried that everyone wouldn't get there in time, like last time. I hadn't eaten anything yet so I made a kale, fruit and yogurt smoothie. I knew I would need the energy for labor but didn't feel like eating anything heavy.

By about noon the contractions were taking all my concentration without much time in between. I told Roy to start filling the pool and told my kids to please clean up the house. Roy hooked up the hose to the shower and began filling the pool. My youngest boy, Armando, helped daddy and then he, Aria and Safire sat watching it fill. I changed into my bikini, stopping to lean forward on something while breathing through each contraction but I was having a hard time relaxing because I was still anxiously waiting for everyone to get there.

My friend Pia arrived just before 1pm. I brought the towels out by the pool, feeling ready to get in already. Another contraction came on and I leaned against the piano. Pia offered to put pressure on my lower back and that gave me instant relief and relaxation. I was so grateful she was there! I listened to the baby's heartbeat with the doppler. It was about the same as before, 130 bpm.

I got into the pool at about 1pm. It wasn't finished filling yet, only covered part of my belly but the water was soothing. Aria and Safire had been waiting anxiously in their swimsuits and were excited to get in the pool with me. Roy was heating pots of water on the stove and adding them to the pool. I labored there in the water with my two little girls playing happily around me. It brought back memories of my first water birth, in labor with Aviana (baby #6) and having little Serina and RJ (my 2 oldest) in the pool with me. I loved letting my kids be a part of it. They swam around splashing and giggling but when a contraction came on I simply let them know "mommy is having a contraction now" and their little voices would become hushed as I leaned against the side, closing my eyes, and focusing inward. I breathed slowly, relaxing and releasing tension, allowing each contraction to pass through me like a gentle wave. When I opened my eyes after the next wave was over, my Serina was there! I hugged her, feeling so happy and relieved that she made it! She has been present for all of her siblings' births, (except for RJ's because she was only 1 year old). She was my first little doula, supporting and comforting me during my labors.

Finally by about 2pm, everyone had arrived! I felt relieved. Everything was happening just as I had hoped and envisioned. Labor was picking up in intensity but I was calm and in control. My sister Cierra leaned over the side to rub my back. I decided Roy should come in the pool with me now so he could better reach me. I wanted pressure on my lower back. Cierra helped get the girls out, wrapping them each in a towel. They put on a movie for them in the bedroom where all the kids were gathered playing card games.

Roy got in the pool with me. His touch was comforting. My oldest son RJ set up the video camera for me and helped scoop some water out of the pool with a big pot because it was really full. I got up on my knees to reposition. I could feel the baby squirming around a lot, probably getting into a better position too! I leaned forward onto the side of the pool, having Roy put pressure on my lower back through each wave. Cierra brought me sips of my home made 'labor aid' or water periodically. I began to feel the baby moving lower. Serina and Pia laid out all the birth pads on the floor in front of the pool and gathered birth supplies. I asked Roy to squeeze my hips as the intensity was building. I said out loud, "It's getting close." I felt a bit of nervous excitement, mixed with the fear of impending pain - the feelings that come along with the rush of adrenaline during transition. I had to remind myself multiple times, 'I've done this 9 times already, I can do it again.' I breathed slowly, swaying my hips, relaxing my face, releasing any tension. I told the kids they should probably come out soon and they soon began trickling quietly out of the bedroom.

The next wave came on and I felt my body beginning to push involuntarily. Pia grabbed my hand, noticing the change. I squeezed her hand and hugged the side of the pool moaning as the pressure was building until I felt a little 'pop' as my water broke (again) followed by a feeling of relief. 'Baby is definitely coming now!', I thought. My water broke at about 2:30, after an hour and a half in the pool. After that wave passed I had Roy take my bikini bottoms off. I was ready to get out but another wave came quickly. I got up on my knees, took a sip of water and another came. Roy squeezed my hips and Cierra held my hand. I knew it was getting so close and I wanted to birth outside the water. I stood up slowly and Roy and Cierra helped me step out and dry off.

I got out of the pool just after 2:30. I asked for my birth ball to lean on. Roy continued putting pressure on my lower back and Cierra held my hand. I spread my knees wide and asked Roy to put the warm washcloth on my perineum. My Mom began helping to apply pressure to my lower back. It was wonderful to have so much support. I really felt like I needed it this time! All the kids had gathered in the living room by this time, quietly, patiently awaiting their baby sibling's arrival. Safire, our 2 year old, quietly came up close to daddy for a few minutes and then sat back on the couch with her big sisters.

The contractions were coming a little slower now. I waited with eyes closed, resting between the waves, allowing my body to do the work. Slowly, gently with each wave my baby was moving down, a little at a time. No rush. I opened my eyes and looked across the room to meet the eyes of my children. "Baby is almost here!" I said softly as I smiled. And then closed my eyes again. I moaned softly as my body began pushing again. I knew baby was coming now and I moved more upright to allow gravity to assist.

I pushed just a little as I felt the intensity of the head crowning. 'This is the hardest part and we're almost there!' I reminded myself. Then I paused, thinking the head was out - but then was surprised when they told me "The head's almost out." So I pushed a little harder and the head was born! I was so anxious to see and touch my baby! I looked down and saw dark hair and a little ear. I reached down and held my baby's head in my hand. It was so slippery and silky soft. It was such an amazing moment, touching my baby while between worlds!

Roy had his hands ready to catch and asked me to take some deep breaths and so I did. I breathed. I waited. Her head was there but her body didn't just slip out right after as it did with most of my others. I moved my hips around a little. A minute and a half went by. Finally, I felt the urge to push and so I began to push and was a bit surprised that I had to push so hard to birth her shoulders. She was born half way still in her amniotic sac. Once her shoulders and arms were out, she slipped slowly into her daddy's hands. I heard her cough and let out a little cry as I turned and sat back against the pool. I lifted my leg as he passed her under and then I saw my baby for the first time! She was a little purple but breathing and I saw right away, it was a GIRL! Our 8th daughter!

She was born at 2:56 pm. Roy lifted her onto my tummy. We did it!! She let out a few little cries and her sisters and brothers moved in close to see her. My mom was crying. Everyone was full of joyful excitement and awe. It was such a beautiful emotional moment to be shared by so many. "Another beautiful baby girl" I said, holding her close. She was perfect. I wiped some bubbles from her mouth and we covered her with a little blanket. She just looked up at me. She was calm. She pinked right up. She was so pretty, with dark hair and cute little lips. She looked just like she did in a dream I had a few days before she was born!

Aria and Safire came up to see her and touch her. Everyone just sat admiring her and chatting. About 20 minutes after birth I offered the breast to her and she latched on pretty quickly. I felt like the placenta was ready. I had felt a couple of contractions while sitting there. As soon as I felt another one, I got up on my knees and Cierra brought the bowl and put it under me. I held my nursing baby in one arm, supporting myself with the other arm while I pushed to birth the placenta into the bowl. It came pretty easily and I sat back down, glad to be done. The placenta took just under 30 minutes. Much faster than last time! I didn't bleed much. I kept baby attached to her placenta. Nana Bea and Tata Roy arrived, happy to see their newest grand baby. Nana Bea was surprised to see the placenta in the bowl. Since her own babies were born in the hospital, she had never even seen a placenta. How crazy is that?!

I took off my wet bikini top so we could have better skin to skin contact and nursed her on the other side. Pia and Cierra helped me get settled on the couch, brought me food, and helped me to the bathroom. I didn't have any tears. There wasn't a whole lot of bleeding and I didn't even have any blood to clean from my legs or anything so I didn't feel the need to shower. What a clean birth!

We took some pictures of the baby with her umbilical cord still attached to her placenta then got ready to cut the cord. The cutting of the cord, the separation of baby from placenta, always feels so sentimental and ceremonial to me. Aria had said that she wanted to cut the cord but decided last minute that she didn't want to. So instead, she helped by cutting the string that we tied the cord with before cutting. So big sister Sara cut the cord. It was about 3 and a half hours after birth.

Then we weighed her. She was 8 pounds 6 ounces! My 2nd

biggest girl. Only Skye and the two boys were bigger. She was my first and only baby in the 8-pound range! AND my very first baby to be born in the middle of the day! Quite a few surprises for me.

Daddy held her and then all the kids took turns holding her. Aunts, uncles and some cousins all came to meet our new baby and help us celebrate her birth. It is our tradition to have a 'zero birthday party' for our new baby. It is fun for the kids. The girls made brownies and we put a zero candle on it. We sang happy birthday to our new baby and Aria and Safire blew out the candle for her.

We all visited, ate brownies and ice cream, and discussed name ideas for the baby. It was Serina that suggested the name Azalea. I liked it and the meaning was a desert flower. We didn't decide on her name that night but we threw some ideas out there. We liked Tierra because it means 'earth' in Spanish and we wanted an earthy name and it rhymes with her Aunt Cierra's name, who held a special place during her birth. It was getting late then so everyone headed home and we headed for bed for our first night with our new little member of the family.

Her birth went just as perfect as it could have! I was so grateful, so happy and so thankful to have been surrounded by so much love and support! It made my heart happy to have all my children there to witness their baby sister's arrival and for them to see and know birth for the normal yet amazing, powerful and beautiful event that it is.

Such an amazing journey it has been from the peaceful

unassisted home birth of my 1st baby at only 19 years old with only my husband and I, to the wonderfully supported family birth of my 10th baby at 40 years old surrounded by all 9 of baby's siblings, my husband, sister, mother and father, as well as, (for the 1st time) a couple of dear friends.

I actually got my 10th baby!! When I was little I always said I wanted to have 10 kids. After we got married I decided that 10 wasn't really a 'realistic number,' but turns out, my childhood dream became my reality after all. I feel that our family is finally complete. Although a family isn't something that is really ever "complete" as it is ever evolving, changing and growing. We are now in this incredible phase where we have adult children, teens, kids, toddlers and a baby all at once! I've been SO blessed to get to experience the beauty of unhindered birth and this special, fleeting newborn phase so many times but I am also beginning to look forward to the next phase of our family growth involving our children bringing in spouses and then - grandbabies!

Celeste

Our unassisted waterbirth

I like to believe labor started a week prior to the day.

Sunday, 4:30 a.m. I woke up to pee and shortly after felt a subtle wave of contraction. Realizing after a few, I wasn't falling back asleep, I recognized again, that this was exactly how my previous two labours began. Could it be time? I didn't want to wake my husband Chris up just yet but he happened to roll over and see that I was up.

I let him know I was having consistent contractions but "wasn't sure if it was time." He reminded me that I said the same thing with our last birth up until the baby was practically out. We laughed about it. We laid together. We talked through each contraction. It was such a sweet time that I won't forget we had. It started getting light out and through the peace and anticipation, I told him we may as well get some sleep. He gave me a kiss and was out in no time. Eventually the waves of contractions carried me to sleep and after a few hours of rest, they completely stopped. We would spend the entire next week together as four. Lunch dates, last minute errands, and celebrating our oldest daughter's birthday that she insisted must happen BEFORE the baby comes. We all laughed at one point during the week saying, "How about Monday? Monday sounds like a good day to have a baby."

Sunday May 9th around 9:30 p.m:

I had a beautiful Mother's Day with the girls. I kissed them both good night that evening knowing it may be one of the last nights with just us. Our oldest had even jokingly spoke to my belly saying, "ok, you can come now!" I laid with our 5 year old girl a little longer after she fell asleep and quietly talked to the baby, as I always did. This time saying, "Ok baby... Mama is ready to do this. Whenever you are ready, your family is waiting to welcome you into the world"... I felt a great sense of calmness. As if I hadn't known I wasn't entirely ready until then.

11:05 p.m. Laying in bed with Chris next to me and just as if baby knew.. I felt my first contraction.

11:45 pm

I told Chris to sleep... this time, downplaying how intense these contractions were starting to feel... Truthfully, I wanted some time to labour on my own. I've only ever laboured on my own. I desired the solitude to get out of my mind and into the place where I meet the peace that only God can give me. 6 hours I let the wave take me in and out of surges, strong enough this time to keep me awake. Until I accepted that these waves needed more of my attention. I woke Chris up and he knew it was time. From the moment he got up, he was right in there for everything I needed. He brought a sense of protection, preparedness and watchfulness to our birth that I can't fully explain.

I was feeling a lot of pressure in my back. I leaned over the bed as Chris would rush to my side ready to bring relief. My bowels were clearing on and off between contractions and I could see faint amounts of bloody show.

Finally, the pool was full enough. Water will always be my therapy. I was ready to allow these strong waves to be held by the warm stillness it brought. Contractions were proving to be stronger each time. Chris would read my sounds to remind me to soften my jaw and breathe from deep down in my lungs. At one point, he had me cradled in his arms, swaying me back and forth in the warm water. Almost as if he was getting as close to taking on the pain for me as he could. Somehow, I was able to go from withstanding the sheer intensity each wave brought one minute, to smiling at Chris and my 5 year old, listening to my music, and having all awareness that this space held no fear. Without any knowledge of how dilated I was, whether or not my waters had burst yet, birth was unfolding. Each wave bringing me closer to shore. Then I wondered, just how far away was that shore? And then, as with each of my labours, I encountered that brief but stark moment, as if I'm outside my body looking in… wondering how long I can truly keep going. I'm exhausted. The transient breaks between contractions are getting shorter and shorter. The comfort of the warm water is fading. Chris's words are getting harder to focus on.

I tell him to text my doula. She had been aware I was in labour, already praying for me with excitement in an entirely different country. "Tell her my contractions are 90 seconds long, 3 minutes a part. Where am I at?! Am I getting close?" I said, hoping she would have the clarity I felt I needed. They may not have been the words my mind wanted at the time, but Chris read me her response, that it so vividly brought me right back into my body: "Stop timing. Get out of your head. Be very present. God is with you!" I grabbed Chris's hand and held it tight. I knew these words well and I immediately surrendered all my thoughts and rested in them.

I told Chris I needed neither of us to talk. Through the next 20 minutes, the room was void of all noise but let me tell you it was FULL of peace. It was as if we both felt it so strongly neither of us wanted it gone. I don't remember feeling anything else during this time. Chris noticed there was some blood in the water. He reached his hand down and gently felt what he later described as soft, swollen and widened. He told me it looked like the baby was getting really low. Then I was stricken with a wave so big it literally took my breath away. I tried to speak and my voice was shaking. Transition phase had come...

Immediately I felt the urge to throw my body over the side of the pool to be on my knees. Chris rushed over and wrapped one arm between my legs and one over my sacrum as if he was holding a baby as it emerged through the birth canal. I knew that everything was still happening by design and my uterus was doing the work to guide my baby out. No need to force or push. It was all one intense surge as baby began to descend out. Chris literally cradling the head in one hand and holding onto me tightly with the other so I would feel him, never leaving my side. Just for a moment, the entire world was still.

I didn't believe that the baby's head was actually out already, so Chris just kept telling me how beautiful it was. Seconds later I let out my strongest roar from deep in my lungs as the rest of my baby left my body entirely, so quickly. As the water transitioned our baby from womb to Chris's hands, he guided her up out of the water as her lungs filled with air and she took her first ever breath in this world. We have another girl! I turned around and there she was. Her cry was strong and her arms were boldly waving as I took hold of her and brought her to my chest. The flood of oxytocin pumping through my veins, the ecstatic look in our eyes. We were crying and laughing all at once. We did it. We actually did it!

Chris encouraged me to get her nice and latched so my uterus would keep contracting my placenta out. Sure enough about 20 min later, my body released it. The last remaining piece that had connected me to my baby for months, had left me. Our golden hours followed as the girls met their sister…

Skin on skin on skin, as we all loved on her, watching her study our faces and smell our scents - of those she had only ever heard for so long. Piled in the bed together, we ate breakfast, started thinking of girl names and just held the joy in the room that only new life can bring. I can't possibly describe the energy that was poured into the room, leaving a permanent stain on all our hearts that since linger amongst the day to day moments of all our lives together.

Thank you so much for listening to our story. It means so

much to be able to share it.

Our rainbow baby

Born at home on 6/20 at 9:06 am.

When we found out we were pregnant in May, it was a surprise but we were so excited. I had been researching home births and knew that's what I wanted to do. I wasn't comfortable going unassisted so I reached out to a midwife group. Fast forward, I unfortunately had a loss at 7 weeks in July. My husband and I started trying as soon as we could and we got a positive on 10/9. The only intervention I had early on, was progesterone to prevent a loss.

This was the best pregnancy out of all of them. I have 2 older kids, both dr lead and hospital births. This one was amazing. There was no pressure, no cervical checks, no pressure for any unnecessary testing. Everything was up to me and on my terms. It was so stress free and easy that way. I loved my midwife group, they truly captured the beauty of birth and the power of the female body.

As the days went by I was eager to meet our baby. We decided to wait to find out the gender. At my 39 week appointment all was good and we just talked about meeting our miracle any day.

I woke up the morning of 6/19 a bit grumpy due to being awake entirely too early for no reason. I went downstairs to watch tv and while laying on the couch felt a trickle, I didn't think it was my water but got up and went to the bathroom just in case. As soon as I sat down a gush of fluid happened and I knew it was my water, it just kept coming. I was so excited!! I went upstairs and told my husband my water had broken and started to tear up, I knew our baby was coming.

I took a shower and we went about our day, got some decaf coffee, a breakfast burrito and walked. I was having tightness but no contractions I could feel. We had the older kids get their stuff ready to go to our families house and let them know my water had broken and we would be in touch when things picked up. Fast forward to the afternoon still on contractions I could feel, still leaking, just enjoying the day. We did a lot of walking, played cards with our friends and just relaxed. The older kids got picked up around 4 and my husband and I watched tv.

Around 7 pm we checked in with the midwife as my water had been broke for 12 hours and she reassured us to just keep hanging on and try and relax and sleep. We went to bed around 10pm, I woke up at 1am feeling contractions but was able to go back to sleep until 4 am when I couldn't sleep through them anymore. I just laid in bed and relaxed and breathed through them until my husband woke up at 5. At that point we got up and started prepping what wasn't prepped already, put on a movie and just hung out while timing the surges. Around 6:30 they were about 5 min apart, lasting for a minute. I wanted to wait until 7 to alert the midwives. The surges were getting more difficult at that point and harder to talk through. At 6:45 my husband decided to page the midwives. They said let's give it another hour and check in but all was good and things were progressing. Almost as soon as the call was done the surges got a lot more intense and closer together. I wasn't able to talk through the surges anymore and was moaning and swaying through them all.

At 7:30 my husband called the midwives back and said they should head on their way, it would take them an hour to get to us. At this point he started filling up the tub and turning on the birthing lights and just getting everything ready last minute, all while coming to help me during the contractions. He was so supportive and amazing I couldn't have done it without him.

Come 8:30 the surges were one on top of each other with little relief in between and I was doing everything I could to ease through them from swaying, to sitting on the toilet, on all fours, even putting my hands in ice to redirect the pain. I hit that "I can't do it" part and my husband reassured me I could and why we were doing this. He called the midwives at this point and asked if I could get into the tub which they said I could. It was too hot though so we had to switch to cold water. I was still in disbelief and worried that labor would stall.

Midwives walked in at 8:42 and I was standing in the pool, it was finally cool enough I could sit down which brought some relief. Around 8:55 they asked if I wanted a cervical check and I said yes even though I was worried they would tell me I wasn't dilated. This was the only check I got and I was fully dilated woohoo. About 5 min later FER kicked in and I told everyone I needed to push, as I was saying this my body just started pushing. It was so crazy I had no control at this point. 2 pushes and my husband said he could see the head. One last giant push and baby was out and into my arms.

We had a beautiful baby boy. My husband and I just sat in the pool holding our son and crying. He never left my arms, once he was born and I didn't tear. He was my biggest baby yet and I didn't tear!! It was amazing. It was the most amazing experience!! As soon as he was born I knew I wanted to do this again and have one more baby, one more homebirth. It was so stress and intervention free. If I had gone the hospital route I knew they would have made me get induced Sunday and not let my body do what it is made to do.

Our son was born at 9:06 weighing 8lbs 5oz and 21 inches long. He was born so healthy and has remained whole and without interventions.

Meaghan Cooley

The Birth of "Freddie"

In July 2020 we decided it was time to start trying for another baby. Over the last few months I had been delving into conscious conception. I had always felt this baby's presence around me and we had already had his name come through very clearly. My husband is Finnish and French Canadian. We felt a strong connection to his name. I had been having dreams of this spirit baby. The day my husband finally said he was ready to start trying was the day we conceived, under a full moon. It was pretty magical. I almost instantly knew I was pregnant.

My first son was born in the hospital system, it wasn't as traumatic as some of the other stories you hear but it certainly wasn't what I had envisioned. I knew things could be different for the next baby. I was determined to give birth at home. I had a very clear vision of the birth from very early on and my mantra throughout was "I trust my body and my baby"

I had found my doula, Jess Quain around the time I was consciously conceiving. I contacted her briefly before we started trying and then again at 6 weeks into the pregnancy and we commenced our journey together. Initially my husband was very against having a freebirth. He was very firm that he wanted someone medical present.

I have been obsessed with birth since having my first son. I had even studied and done a doula course. Over time, by educating and perseverance I was able to shift his mindset. He came full circle and was incredibly supportive. We had to have many discussions including one where I told him that if he wasn't ok with me birthing at home, he couldn't be there. I didn't want any fear in the birth space. We did a lot of work with our beautiful doula leading up to the birth. He released his fear and it was amazing to see him change into a position of unwavering support.

I was steadfast in my vision for my birth. I did a lot of journaling and whenever a fear would come up I did a lot of work to release and understand the fear and why I may be experiencing it. I still had some trepidation going into the birth but I believe a healthy amount of nerves is to be expected.

The night before I went into labour, our son Hugo was sleeping over at my parents house for the night. I was feeling emotional. I felt huge and over it and had a bit of an emotional meltdown. I cried and cried while Erik held me and listened. I went to bed and actually had a reasonable restful sleep. I woke feeling like I had cleared something by crying and releasing it all out.

That morning as I lay in bed I felt a little twinge at around 9 am. Nothing painful but a cramping sensation. I dismissed it. I was induced with my first so I had no idea what to expect for a physiological labour. I had also been over analyzing every bodily sensation and googling "how will I know when I am in labour."

Around 10 minutes later the sensation started again. I was still unconvinced and unexcited. Throughout the pregnancy I had experienced pelvic instability and I assumed that it could be another flare up of pain. I got out of bed and decided to go do a little bit of shopping. I bought a tin of pineapple as I had read that it could induce labour. I didn't end up eating it.

At the shops I was on a mission and was very focused. Get in. Get out. I could feel some sensations at the shop but I was in denial. I got home and asked Erik to start a fire because it was the first cold day for the year. We have an open fireplace which is such a lovely addition to our home. He chopped some wood while I dropped into my body. He started the fire and as it was burning I remember feeling like it was so primal. It was very quiet and ritualistic. I sat on my bouncy exercise ball and watched the fire for a bit. I felt some more surges but still wasn't convinced that I was in labour. I put on my labour playlist and we sat together quietly with our dogs watching the fire.

When I was sitting down and relaxing the surges would stop. I walked around to see what would happen and sure enough things would ramp up again. I ate some lunch and around 1pm my mum returned with Hugo. She took one look at me and said that I was definitely in labour. I laughed and dismissed it. Then a surge came and I had to close my eyes and pay full attention. I asked Erik to heat up my wheat bag. My mum left and our darlin Hugo was demanding full attention but my contractions were getting stronger. We made the decision to call Erik's mum who was going to take Hugo when I was in labour. Erik left to drop him off at 3pm. When Erik returned he got a call from his mates inviting him out to dinner. I told him to go and that I wasn't in labour. He looked at me like I was crazy. I was still in denial.

The day before, my girlfriend had arrived from WA for a visit. She popped over and braided my hair for me as I sat on the bouncy ball. At this stage I was unable to talk through contractions. I asked Erik to run the bath. I was ready to hop in. This was around 3:30pm.

Throughout the bathroom and the house I had put up my Bearthling's affirmation cards. I asked my girlfriend to help me set up the space. She got all of my alter crystals that my girlfriends had gifted me at my mother blessing and we set them up in a grid on the sink. I love my bathroom. It's full of plants and it feels really nice in there. My friends had written down words of encouragement, which were up in the bathroom.

At around 4pm I got into the bath. My girlfriend made me a cup of tea. I sank into the water and concentrated. In between contractions I asked Erik to call Jess our Doula. She had gone to Rosebud for the weekend. She could hear me over the phone and dropped what she was doing and came. I had also spoken to my girlfriend Chloe and she wanted to come. She had expressed her desire to become a doula too. We talked about how amazing it would be if my birth was the initiation for her into the birth world.

The surges were coming regularly and were getting stronger. Chloe arrived and gently kissed my arms. I relaxed knowing she was there. I could feel the presence of my other girlfriend who was studying in our living room. Feminine energy is so powerful in those moments.

I was so focused and in between a surge I would be able to ask for something. As it was light outside, I asked Erik to "turn the sun off," so he put up bed sheets over the windows. This was a massive help. I would open my eyes after a massive surge, have a sip of water, look at an affirmation card and then take its message with me into the realm of labour. It took all of my mental capacity to focus and breathe throughout. At about 5:30pm I wanted to get out of the bath.

We all went into the bedroom. I remember this stage feeling very primal. I felt a bit of fear as my whole body worked hard with each surge. I sat on the floor with my legs apart and my waters broke all over the carpet. The waters were clear which was a relief. I could not get comfortable. I was throwing my body around, trying to find a comfortable position that would help. Erik would hold me up but then I would push him away as it was so intense. Jess was on speakerphone coaching us all through it. Chloe would gently come up and remind me to breathe which was so helpful. In hindsight I was obviously in transition. I felt like I couldn't do it anymore. I kept repeating "I can't do it anymore" and everyone would hold the space for me and remind me that I could do it and I was doing it.

I felt like I needed to open my bowels. Jess realised what was happening and told me to go sit on the toilet. I got to the toilet and roared. This was so intense. I sat there for a few seconds before deciding I wanted to get back into the bath. The bath was still lovely and warm, Chloe and Erik helped me in. I roared again and was on my knees with my head resting on the side of the bath. Jess arrived at this point.

I felt between my legs and couldn't feel anything significant. I felt my anus and it felt like it was prolapsing which was a bit of a shock. I roared again and did a huge involuntary push. I looked down and could see his head in between my legs. I remember having a moment of stillness and wonder how incredible that was. I reached down and touched his head. I then felt his body rotate. I felt another surge and with that his body was born. He was earthside.

I was in a bit of shock and didn't even think to pick him up. Jess gently said, "Pick him up." I brought him to my chest and he let the air into his lungs with a cry. Born at 1803 under a new moon.

We stayed in the bath for about 10 minutes, just marveling at him and how I had just done what I set my heart on. I decided to get out, as the bath was getting cooler. Everyone helped us get out and we waddled to the couch.

We were in the magical hour of enchantment. I couldn't stop staring at him. I remember the look of awe on my husband's face. He was so amazed and impressed that I had achieved my dream birth. Our little Freddie was perfect. Meanwhile Jess and Chloe put some washing on and cleared up. Chloe left soon after with a look on her face that I will never forget. Awe. Jess looked at us and suggested hopping into bed where we would be more comfortable.

As I was climbing into bed my placenta literally fell out with a wet plop. Jess and I laughed. It had been a concern of mine that it wouldn't come out.

Jess was sneakily taking photos of us all together. Freddie did the breast crawl and had his first feed. Jess made us food and cups of tea, she was invaluable. I will never forget how amazing she was.

At about 8pm I felt like Freddie was ready to be cut from his cord. It was a feeling that he communicated to me. Jess had got us a beautiful cord tie from Blissful Herbs, a local herbalist. Erik tied the tie and cut the cord. We kept the placenta to bury under our passionfruit vine. The passion fruit, as I type this some months later, is absolute.

Felicity

Basking with my bundle of boys

I'd been experiencing little, growing twinges in the few weeks leading up to the birth. Lots of warm up tightenings in my uterus, soft bowel movements, one random bout of vomiting, hormonal surges, emotional changes, gentle menstrual cramping. It was kinda hard not to focus on each little progression towards labour, wondering if each one would be a 'sign' that I would look back on in hindsight. My first two births, both freebirths, the mucus plug and waters releasing were clear signs that labour was about to start, so I was looking out for these obvious bodily messages. But these didn't come! Something different was in store.

Instead, I woke as per nearly usual, around 4am needing a wee. I got out of bed, feeling a little discomfort which again had now been the norm in the final weeks, did my wee then got back in. Except things felt a bit funny. I suddenly had very deep ache on one side of my lower back and in my abdomen, and felt the need to hurry back to the loo. I had a thorough clear out of my bowels, still actually in denial that this was labour starting. But then I just knew that this was a bit different, so woke my husband and we went downstairs together.

112

I immediately found solace sitting on the downstairs toilet, and asked him to set up the birth pool; things had begun to open up and though I don't time my surges, I knew that they were starting to ramp up a gear quite quickly. My last labour was 1.5hrs so I knew things might well happen very quickly!

I was able to get in a comfy position on the loo. Sure enough, surges were coming thick and fast, and I would focus on breathing through each one; deep breaths in, and slow, focused breaths out. I found a kind of hypnotic state to breathing too; rolling my breaths in and out, with loose lips blowing out, was really helping me ride the waves. Just before a surge, I'd feel a burst of hormones and enter into a blissful high, ready to ground and float into each surge. The times between each one was shortening quickly. I could feel myself opening fast, and movement downwards. There was so much pressure inside, and I was holding my pubic mount giving myself counter pressure whilst circling my hips through each surge, which really helped.

My husband let me know the birth pool was ready to get into. I'd been having thoughts that the baby could even be born on the toilet, so I was relieved to hear that I had a pool of water waiting for me. I took my chance to stand and move to the next room in between surges, and into the partially filled pool and Oh. My. God. The water was utterly blissful. Instant relief! I immediately went on all fours, using the seat as a support, and my husband hosed my back gently with the warm running water. Heaven!

The surges were increasing again, and all throughout, the

pain in my back was increasing. During each one, there was intense pressure in my pubic mount and the right hand lower side of my back. I'd felt that baby had started labour on my right hand side, and the feelings in my back were similar to when they'd stay on the right during pregnancy. I'd also guessed that possibly baby was coming out posterior, as this labour just felt so so different to my other two. Pain this time, and in my back, whereas previously it was just intense sensations and mostly in my abdomen.

So far I'd been able to breathe through each surge, using movements in my hips to gently help things move. I started to get really hot, so my husband brought a cool flannel and some apple juice that I sipped. A few more intense surges, and then suddenly I was able to come up for air in between, for the first time in a while. I was able to rest my head on the side of the pool, even had a little chat and giggle with my husband. Then things started back up again with a severe intensity, and I was back in the zone.

I asked my husband to get in the pool and apply pressure to my lower back as it was so sore, so we were both applying pressure to my body at this point. I knew that baby must be close, but I wasn't quite bearing down. I started to feel worried that things were going to take ages, and that maybe I needed the help of a midwife, that I wasn't able to do this, etc. Turns out, at the same time, my husband also had some personal fears rise, unbeknownst to me. I had entered the transitional stage, and so did he! I recognised the feeling of transition and at that point knew that I must be close, which was a relief. So I gathered myself mentally, and knew that there was only one way out the other side of this birthing experience and that was straight through the middle.

Sure enough, I started to feel the onset of bearing down. At this point, breathing wasn't cutting it and I started to make the other worldly birthing noises that come from the pure depths of somewhere else. I was roaring, howling almost; lion and wolf as one. It felt so painful and releasing sounds felt so cathartic. I willed my body to open and release, knowing that everything was okay, just sore. I felt an urge to touch my clitoris and the stimulation felt good. I relaxed. I allowed myself to relax and to feel my yoni. I could feel the start of the baby's head. I knew I wasn't tearing, though my whole being felt like it was being ripped open.

A few more powerful surges and my body released the baby's head into the water! Wow!! I held the head, and though I could feel hair, it felt different to the last water birth that I'd had. And then I remembered that my waters still hadn't released, and that the baby was still inside their amniotic sac; a baby born en caul! I'd dreamed about that, literally! I held the head as my body surged again and as the baby came, the waters released and my baby was here!

I gently lifted them out of the water, on to my chest and sank back into my husband's arms! The feeling like no other! Relief, euphoria, hard work paid off! Wow!!!!!

I cuddled my babe and they gently cleared their lungs, making a little cry but otherwise so so peaceful. The most gentle transition! From when I woke to when they were born was 2.5 hrs, cushioned in the amniotic sac, born into water.

I sat in the birth pool, surrounded by birth blood and membranes and juice and everything else, in total awe. A quick check on baby to make sure everything was okay, and I relaxed in the water. A few minutes later, our toddler woke up so papa went upstairs to bring him down. His face was in shocked reverence when he came through the door, silently watching the magical scene before him. "What's that?" he asked. "It's your new baby brother!" I replied. At this point, my husband and I grinned at each other; thinking I'd been carrying a girl, we were now parents to a bundle of boys!

The placenta hadn't arrived yet and I was aware to keep things super relaxed to help it come. In my previous births, the placenta had been rushed and there had been stress and fear involved, so I was determined to have a different experience this time. I was feeling my uterus contract, but wasn't feeling stable reclining or sitting in the birth pool, so I decided to slowly come out. The slight anxiety building from not feeling comfy was soon released as my husband reminded me there's absolutely no rush, and he prepared towels and pads on the sofa.

I had a feeling the placenta might come as soon as I moved, so he came over prepared with the bowl. Sure enough, he held baby and as I stood up, my uterus contracted and out fell the placenta! 45 mins after birth, all intact, and straight in the bowl. I was helped out of the pool and sat on the sofa with baby and placenta; it felt good to be on dry land at this point!

My husband had been, yet again, the most incredible birth partner I could ever dream of. He prepared, held, and kept the birth space in the most perfect way. Instinctively just knowing what was needed, I barely had to use words. He felt me and the baby on such a deep level and I felt totally and utterly safe and loved and respected and cared for. His praises need shouting from the rooftops!

My husband went to wake up our eldest, who slept through the first attempts to wake him and everyone came back in together to say hello. Total love at first sight from biggest brother, who has been saying goodnight to the baby every night for months now. They recognised each other!

We sat and basked in the beautiful vibes for a while; the kids had breakfast, I had an apple and a rest! Super husband and papa continued to do all the things for everybody. Baby started gently rooting for my breast, so I helped him latch and he has been a champ feeder from the very start!

Later on, we felt it was time to perform the fire ceremony with the umbilical cord, so out came the special candles we'd bought. We chanted a sacred mantra as mama, papa and biggest brother held candles to sever the cord. It was beautiful and gentle, and for us, more practical than the lotus birth we'd had first time around.

Mama and baby were then helped gently upstairs into bed and after some breakfast, it was time to sleep!

Leonie

Of course you did it

I felt sensations begin at around 12:30am. By 2:30, I could no longer stay in bed and woke up my husband. Being 39 weeks, I was mentally prepared to go to 42+, so even during these strong waves, I told my husband the surges might go away. During the short process of gathering last-minute things like a bowl for the placenta and a couple towels, I had to stop every couple of minutes to breathe through a sensation. I was still present and talking and joking in between but that shifted quickly. I soon wanted my husband to squeeze my hips. One of the times I was stepping out of the bathroom, I knelt down and never got back up. I was no longer here, even in between sensations.

My husband sat behind me, hardly saying anything, just completely present. I was vocalizing through the sensations, having a dialogue of conversation in my head. "Wow, this is really picking up," followed by, "You haven't even begun." My hips were circling and burning like I have never experienced. There was so much internal pressure and my body began pushing at the end of each wave, with so much intensity pulling me under the surface.

I was waiting for my waters to release, but they never

did. I noticed some blood on the towel under my knees but I wasn't worried at all. While I was still experiencing involuntary pushing urges, growing in intensity, my husband said he could see the sac bulge with our son inside. I roared and his head was born. I waited and breathed. He birthed his shoulders on the next contraction and tumbled out just after 4:30am.

James calmly unlooped the cord from around the baby's neck and handed him to me through my legs. He gave a little cry and I sucked some fluid from his mouth and nose and he began to wail. My husband asked if he needed anything and I said, "No, he's perfect." I was in complete disbelief and our two toddlers slept through the whole thing.

I said, "I can't believe I did it!" And my husband said, "Of course you did it."

My placenta was born 5 hours later and we've been in a bubble of pure bliss ever since.

Nicki

The birth of Beorn

I had been having prodromal labor for over 2 weeks with my contractions picking up in intensity and frequency every evening/night. On the night of the Nov 30th they felt different and I knew babe would be arriving soon. The contractions remained through the night and all throughout the next day. I worked remotely all day but I also took it easy, taking a walk with my daughter, bouncing on the birth ball and watching a movie.

Around 5pm on the 1st they picked up to every 5 min and started getting more intense and radiated mainly in my back. We migrated upstairs to start setting up the room. We had just finished putting up the birth pool and filling it when Leah, my doula, arrived. We just enjoyed talking and Arwen (my 2.5 yr daughter) kept coming over and asking questions. We danced on and off between contractions. Soon it was time for her to go to bed and I started to concentrate a bit more on laboring as I was having serious back contractions by that point.

I sent Aaron and my MIL downstairs to watch tv, to allow me some quiet. Aaron would come up and check on me occasionally to see how things were progressing. There was a chaise lounge in my room that was just the right height to lean on for contractions in our room. Leah was wonderful in providing counter pressure through my back labor and reminding me to release tension. I tried out the tub but I couldn't seem to get comfortable since the pains were so focused in my back. It just didn't feel right.

I moved to labor on the toilet for a while and my contractions picked up in frequency and intensity. I loved and hated that toilet because I knew it was helping but the contractions were so painful I really had to concentrate and remind myself to release the tension and let my body work. Any time I felt the tension, I would breathe through and release it and it would help my pain level so much. I knew transition was nearing and told Leah. She said she didn't think I was there yet but to trust my body.

I knew we were close so I decided it was time to get in the tub. Just as I expected, a few minutes later, I felt a major shift and a pop as my water broke in the tub. Immediately contractions got very intense. Aaron came in to check since he could audibly hear me moaning through each contraction. The doula told him that I was in transition and he should stick around. A few moments later, I could feel the baby's head and told Aaron to wake Arwen because the baby was coming. He went and got her and they both came in just as FER kicked in. I could feel the baby's head coming out but I was in an awkward position.

I felt the need to adjust in the tub from being on my knees to sitting on my bottom and as soon as I did, I had a contraction and the baby's body quickly came out. I scooped him out of the water. There was no blood at all. The baby was very clean with very little vernix. Born at 11:39pm on Dec 1st.

I held the baby on my chest rubbing and patting its back to help it get the fluid out. He was a bit limp and not very responsive. Someone asked if it was a boy or girl and I told them that they would need to wait. Once he let out a few cries and I could tell he was breathing, I looked and saw that it was a boy! A wave of joy and relief came over me as I hugged my boy and thanked God for bringing him to us safely. We named him Beorn Caspian James Scarbro.

Then I got out of the tub and moved to the bed. Arwen cuddled with me and baby Beorn for a little while until she started looking sleepy and Aaron took her back to bed. Once Aaron returned I got out of bed to birth the placenta, 45 minutes after birth. There was a small gush of blood with the placenta but not too much. I felt great, there was no tearing and I didn't really have any pain down there.

I was amazed at how wonderful I felt. About 90 min after birth we did the cord burning. It was a slow peaceful process as we all took turns holding the candles that separated him from his last connection to the womb.

We weighed and measured him - 7lb 4oz and 20.5in long. Then we all settled in to rest.

Hannah Scarbro

The unassisted birth of Skye

I want to mention that Homebirth on Your Own Terms was my sole resource, apart from listening to a few podcast episodes, and I appreciated it so much!

Around 6am on the 8th of August, I woke up to gentle cramping sensations. I had told my husband the week before that I thought the baby would come on this day and even though my official "due date" was August 12th. I had been telling others it was the 8th... as though I thought I could wish or will it into existence.

I had planned this free birth since the beginning of the year when we knew we were moving to Sioux Falls, South Dakota. After what seemed to me like an extensive internet search on home birth midwives in the area, I had come to my own conclusion that there were only "medwives" and that I would need to find an alternative solution to birthing my baby outside of the hospital system (a conclusion that I would later discover was false but at that point my heart was all in for a free birth).

This would be my third birth. With my first I had a terrible and unnecessary induction which I will spare the details right now but after this completely disempowering experience, I grieved what could have been and was left with a heart full of regrets. With my second, we used a midwife and it was an entirely beautiful experience and everything I needed at the time.

Shortly after waking in the morning of August 8th, the waves of pressure were quickly intensifying and I started to prepare myself. I was convinced that the baby was coming that day. As my husband and two toddlers were still sound asleep in their beds, I began setting up our master bathroom with everything I had been collecting for this day... a few tinctures, old towels, a shower curtain liner, umbilical cord clamp, sterile scissors, amongst a few more odds and ends.

I walked into the kitchen to where my phone was charging on the counter and decided it was time to tell my mother, who had planned to make the three hour journey from Minnesota to help us out with the toddlers, upon baby's arrival. By this time it was nearly 7am and I confidently told her that the baby was coming today but to take her time as I was just starting labor.

I went back into the bathroom and started swaying and moving my hips with the deep sensations that were getting stronger. I downloaded a free contraction app and timed a couple contractions but quickly abandoned it as I remembered why I hated doing this upon the advice of my midwives with the second child. My contractions have always been intense and close together—shorter and not fitting the traditional patterns of labor. It was useless.

Around 7:30am I could see that my husband was stirring to wake so I nudged him and let him know it was baby day. By this time our other two littles were also starting to wake and my husband began tending to them as I pained and swayed in the bathroom. I let him know I now thought the baby was arriving fast because I wasn't getting much of a break from the contractions. At one point he came in and asked if I needed anything. I told him that I just needed to be alone for a bit. I remember looking at myself in the mirror and saying, "it is just me and you, baby," as if I knew what was to come.

The contractions were getting more intense and I threw two blankets on the floor in front of the Moroccan pouf that I had brought into the bathroom earlier. I kneeled on the pouf and swayed my body in deep circles with the flowing sensations. I breathed in one earth shattering contraction and with a huge burst my water broke. The blankets I'd put down were now drenched but I was too deep in between worlds to care or do anything about it. At that point nothing existed but me and my baby. The next sensation was so intense that I had no choice but to surrender to the pain. I wiped the sweat from my forehead and rested my head on the soft leather. This was transition.

Then suddenly I felt my eyes widen and the extreme urge to push. I cried out to my husband but the cries seemed muffled as I simultaneously felt as if my entire being was being split in half. I'm still not sure how loud my cries were as part of me was somewhere else in the aether.. but at the same time I was fully here for it. I felt her make her way earthside with a great heaviness as she came down.

And it was on that bathroom floor (in our first house that we had just purchased one month before) that Skye came to earth fast and furious, all at once into my own hands at 8:20am on 8/8/2022 with no one present but she and I. I grasped her tightly, marveling at her tiny perfection as she gave out a healthy cry and then, sleepily shut her eyes tightly—as if she was trying to adjust to her bright, new world from the darkness of the watery womb.

Just then my husband came into the room as we gently untangled the cord from the back of her neck and I held her to my chest. Adrenaline was coursing through my body and at the same time I felt immense peace. An unknown period of time passed as I just sat on that floor with my baby in my arms and delivered the placenta. My husband then put the shower curtain down on our bed where our single birth photo was then taken. I left her cord connected until the blood had fully drained, then my husband attached the clamp and cut it.

She was the perfect birthing partner for what I suspect was my last. She worked with me beautifully to bring herself here, in the most empowering and healing way I could imagine. We named her Skye like the Scottish island and in honor of God's miraculous backdrop in this Earth game.

The Birth of Lilith Mary

The soul of miss Lili came to be at conception of my first pregnancy. I could have sworn over those first weeks that I was pregnant with a girl. Somewhere, several weeks down the line, a shift occurred. It was no longer the spirit of LM I felt within, but a quiet calling of my sweet boy.

Four years later, it was finally time for Lilith to join us earthside. And so she did, under the Flower Supermoon, our little girl began her journey to us in the physical. The entire pregnancy had been extremely challenging managing extreme nausea throughout the entire duration. Morning, noon, or night, I was sick.

By the time Lili was conceived, I had spent several years working within the birth world in some capacity or another. I knew more about the benefits of homebirth and the thought of freebirth, sounded exhilarating. To be in my power, with just my family, in our own home— I couldn't imagine much better. Still, with being so ill and an early delivery with my first, I was cautious. I went to the OB appointments, while fighting for my right to informed choice and decision.

At 34 weeks, my doctor first mentioned an induction. Mind you, she had very little understanding of my nausea and vomiting, and every other test you could do was perfect. I was healthy, baby was healthy. Why were we bringing up induction so early. I had gone into labor spontaneously with my first after all. I brushed it off. I could see the energetic game at play, the small seeds of doubt being planted, and I wasn't going to play. I laughed and joked that it wouldn't be long and she would be here. I was so certain she too would be early.

37 weeks came and went. What was punctuated with braxton hicks slowed to just her wiggles and turns. 38 weeks. 39 weeks. Each time my OB offering the induction. Each time pushing to get it on the schedule on a day she'd be present. I was 40 weeks and walked into, yet another appointment. I broke down, I was so confused, why wasn't it happening? I had been healthy all pregnancy. I was ready to give birth and meet my baby. Something I never thought I'd say. So I scheduled it. I still had days for labor to get started and a heart set on birthing at home.

It was the day before we were scheduled to go in for the induction. I was feeling completely gutted. There were no signs of labor, my dream birth (my last birth experience) was slipping through my fingers. I felt myself being pulled under by the weight of the hospital system and that scheduled induction. I cried a lot that day. And when I had finished crying I remembered my own power. I was physically in good health, there was no real medical reason for me to be induced (outside of their arbitrary due date estimations). My baby was healthy. She was moving, heartbeat strong and steady. I knew we were okay. When I had let everything go, I sat in the nothingness. It was as if every cell in my being stood up in defiance. I could not go to that induction. I would not. And so, I didn't.

I tried calling to let them know I wouldn't be coming in the next morning, my heart pounding. This was it. I was taking ownership of me, my baby and my birth. What followed with the hospital opened up their unorganized disregard for mother's care, but that's not where this story leads.

I was now 42 weeks pregnant. Three days past my scheduled induction. And no signs of labor. At this point, I was still feeling good— I was healthy, baby was moving lots and heartbeat was solid. But the doubt began to creep in. Would I be going to the hospital anyway?

42 weeks and 2 days, we have contractions! I was so excited to finally get the show on the road. I had been trying all of the home induction methods. Sex, dates, spicy foods, self membrane sweeps. I probably bounced on that ball enough to cross the country. It was only, of course, when I let all of that go and disconnected from the world, that labor began.

There were many communications my baby shared with me while in utero. One being her name. Two being her astrological sign, Pisces (which I never thought we'd get to) and a vision of her as a girl running through our garden. So while I didn't know how birth would unfold, I knew her and I would be safe. We would find ourselves running through the sun and flowers in the coming years.

When contractions began, I felt an immediate relief but knew it could be some time. I was in early labor for sometime before my first birth. Even with second births happening faster, I knew there could still be a long while before baby arrived. The first day of early labor was spent with my boys, my partner, son and dog, going for walks, eating our favorite foods and cuddly naps. The contractions would pick up and slow down. I grew impatient with the inconsistency. I had waited all this extra time, I was ready to move past this early stage of labor.

Outside of my partner's presence, we had a birth doula. She was a friend and someone whom I trusted and knew viewed birth as a natural, normal event. She trusted birth, as I trust birth. She came over that first evening to be with us and see where things were at. After continued sporadic contractions we all called it an evening. I wasn't certain if I was going to be able to sleep but found I quickly drifted and slept throughout the night.

The next morning was met with a more certain kind of contraction. Not that the day before weren't real, but they were softer in comparison. We woke up and went about our normal flow. I found myself more distracted by the sensations that I had been the previous day. I also found myself growing a shorter emotional threshold for distractions.

I always dreamed of my son being present at my birth. To see his sister come into the world... not to return home with a new human in my arms. But that morning I knew it couldn't be done, I needed space. More so, I needed to not worry about him while requiring my partners full attention and support as needed. Once my son left, our doula returned 11 a.m. and things were staying consistent.

I was bouncing and rocking on the ball. I was still able to talk and easily breathe through contractions. This is when I lost track of time. I had been too in my head, timing contractions and hoping the labor kept progressing rather than allowing it to happen on its own accord.

"What would you do if you weren't labor?" our doula asked from across the room. I realized I hadn't eaten much in the last day or so. While my partner heated up some food I had prepped for postpartum, I traded off contraction timing and allowed myself to be for a while. Soon after things began to pick up.

I was now standing and needed movement to work through the contractions. Each wave now needed my full attention and my partner's support to lean into. He became my rock. While we danced our way into a more active phase of labor, our doula began filling our birth pool. I had been so on the fence about purchasing one and am so glad I did.

Once in the water I felt the sharp edge of the contractions ease. I could still be the pressure building but it became much more manageable. While in the pool I roared between various positions. Sitting upright, leaning on the pool's edge, laying back, switching positions every so often. I was still present with my doula and partner at this point. Able to continue conversation between contractions but tuning inwards during their duration.

My partner joined me in the pool in the early evening hours. It was such a relief to pull from his strength. We labored that way for a short while, until his legs grew tired... and our pool started leaking. We had gone back and forth on whether or not to bring the trap in from our shed to place under the pool. He had sworn it wouldn't a problem without one. In the moment, all I could do was laugh. I also really needed to use the bathroom and empty my bladder. We used the transition to relieve myself and the pool leaks.

I have worked in birth for several years now. I know the toilet is the birthing station. I tried my hardest to pee in the water out of fear of what the dry land would bring. Once out of the warm, supportive water the contractions became firey, sharp pains. It was almost as if I could feel each muscle of my uterus pulling itself back in preparation to push the baby down and out. it was intense, it felt as though it was one long contraction, one with no end.

The change of events here, is blurry. I got back into the pool and had completely entered the birth portal. I was aware of the room and those in it, but I also felt infinite. Evening had descended upon our house at this time. The candles and lights giving it a warm yellow glow. I shifted between a kneeled position with my forehead resting on the side of the pool and flipping over with my body floating limp in the warm waters. The later provided respite when I needed.

I had done my due diligence when it came to choosing to birth without trained medical assistance. For some reason, what stuck with me most, was not to overexert myself. I rested, and knew, my body would be able to birth without my effort. So when I started to feel "pushy" almost like I could have a bowel movement, and I couldn't feel her head- I recoiled some.

I knew I was making the most progression on my hands and knees, but it was tearing me in that position. The contractions were all encompassing. I tried my best to breathe and moan as felt natural. Floating on my back through several contractions. Part of me knew what was being avoided. I knew what needed to happen, but I also needed this moment to pause. The contractions felt bigger than me. I called upon my ancestors, guardians, female deities and saints. "Be with me now, Carry me through this." Almost instantly, the discomfort lessened. I had found my inner strength to continue.

"Let's try the next one on your knees again," the doula comments from across the room. I'm sure she senses it too. I turn over, both knees firmly planted into the floor, my forehead resting on the inflatable edge. One intense contraction washes over me. Instinctively, I stand up and feel something slip between my pelvis. Quickly my hand moves to my vulva and is met with a round head of hair. "holy shit" I think. Part of me knew she would be born quickly but not in this way. I'm completely within and outside of my body at this point; Having a wild, powerful spiritual experience. I can hear the doula at my right, "it's okay, take your time, breathe." To my left my partner is in complete shock, I can tell he's not certain what to do or how to help. All of this happens within a moment when

I realize that being six feet tall and trying to catch a baby standing might not be the best idea. I come down to one knee. Now, I have a bit of a nerdy side. I'll indulge in some video games and appreciate the mental break they provide. One thought came through my head as my knee met the ground and that was to "Finish this" in the cadence of Mortal Kombat (she admits with embarrassment).

I use the next contraction, or two, to easily bring my baby into this world. There was no "ring of fire" or burning perineum. There was no tearing. No pulling or twisting to get the baby out. In fact, I felt the baby complete its shoulder rotation in that dance we shared through this labor land. As I bring her up to my chest, I gently fall back along the side of the pool. I "had fucking done it." That was all I could think of.

Her cord was over her shoulders slightly and not very long, which made it difficult to comfortably hold her. She quickly cried and loudly made her presence known. She was beautiful and healthy and here at last! At 10:07 am, about twelve hours of active labor and a couple pushes later. That moment was all in one lifetime and a blink of an eye. For the joy and relief of labors end was met with the sharp pains of the placenta.

I felt more discomfort in delivering the placenta than I did my baby. It was very important to me that the sacred postpartum time be honored, it was a huge deciding factor in choosing a homebirth. I deeply believed in allowing my baby the time to take in all of the placental nourishment she could before that was disconnected. As much as I hate to admit it, I didn't check the cord too closely before we cut things. The length of the cord made maneuvering with her difficult and the after pains were increasing. With the baby disconnected I was able to move from the pool and into the bedroom to reunite with my partner and baby.

It had been about twenty minutes post birth and while tugged on the cord, there was still quite a bit of traction meeting my pull. Nursing and the oxytocin rush that followed, would be one way to support the final stage of birth to be completed. To my surprise, she easily latched and began nursing. This caused my contractions to quickly increase but I still found the cord met with resistance and it was nearly 45 minutes after birth. I had purchased a few tinctures after much research and took a dropper full intended to help support the release of the placenta. The tincture worked something magic. After about five or ten minutes, I felt it release from my womb and drop down into the birth canal. I came to a low squat on the side of my bed and as gently as a chicken lays an egg, I pulled my placenta from my body. Like two wild women, my doula and I began looking over the placenta, checking for any missing parts and it's overall condition to be telling of our health. It was beautiful, thick red; a breeding ground of life.

We settled in, my baby and me. The rest of the world faded away. My partner and doula tidied things briefly before he returned to our bed. We missed the cut of for food delivery hours and ate frozen energy balls instead… staring at our newest love. "I can't believe how simple that was" my partner said when all was said and done. After holding so much fear about birthing with our intention and power, he had quickly come to see what I felt to be truth all along.

I'm now only six months postpartum and still see the medicine of this birth taking form in my daily life. There are two that hold the most value. One, is to have patience and trust that everything you dream of can and will come true. And two, always always trust your intuition, it will never lead you into something that is not meant for you.

Resources

Birth Becomes Hers by Bree Moore
The Birth Partner by Penny Simkin
Birth Without Fear by January Harshe
Birth Without Violence by Frederick Leboyer
Birth Your Way by Sheila Kitzinger
Childbirth Without Fear by Grantly Dick-Read
Emergency Childbirth by Gregory White
Gentle Birth Choices by Barbara Harper
Heart and Hands by Elizabeth Davis
Holistic Midwifery by Anne Frye
Homebirth On Your Own Terms by Heather Baker
Orgasmic Birth by Elizabeth Davis and Debra Pascali-Bonaro
Spiritual Midwifery by Ina May Gaskin
The Unassisted Baby by Anita Evensen
Unassisted Homebirth an Act of Love by Lynn Griesemer
Welcome With Love by Jenny Overend
Wise Woman Herbal for the Childbearing Year by Susun Weed

www.unassistedchildbirth.com
www.freebirthsociety.com
www.indiebirth.org
www.spinningbabies.com
www.evidencebasedbirth.com

Contact the Author

Have more questions, want to add your story or birth photos? Would you like to contact the Author? Feel free to do so at heatherbakermw@gmail.com

Future edits for both Home Birth on Your Own Terms and Our Births, Our Stories will have additional room to include YOUR inspirational story.

 amazon.com/Heather-Baker/author/B08TWHC2G5

 heatherbakermidwife

Made in the USA
Coppell, TX
22 April 2023

15921258R00085